The
Complete Single's
Guide to Being a
dog
owner

BETSY ROSENFELD

adamsmedia
Avon, Massachusetts

Published by
Adams Media, a division of F+W Media, Inc.
57 Littlefield Street, Avon, MA 02322. U.S.A.
www.adamsmedia.com

Appendix B contains material adapted and abridged from *The Everything® Puppy Book*,
by Carlo De Vito and Amy Ammen, copyright © 2002 by F+W Media, Inc.,
ISBN 10: 1-58062-576-2, ISBN 13: 978-1-58062-576-0.

ISBN 10: 1-59869-723-4
ISBN 13: 978-1-59869-723-0

Printed in the United States of America.

J I H G F E D C B A

Library of Congress Cataloging-in-Publication Data
is available from the publisher.

This publication is designed to provide accurate and authoritative information with
regard to the subject matter covered. It is sold with the understanding that the publisher
is not engaged in rendering legal, accounting, or other professional advice. If legal
advice or other expert assistance is required, the services of a competent professional
person should be sought.
—From a *Declaration of Principles* jointly adopted by a Committee of the American Bar
Association and a Committee of Publishers and Associations

Many of the designations used by manufacturers and sellers to distinguish their product
are claimed as trademarks. Where those designations appear in this book and Adams
Media was aware of a trademark claim, the designations have been printed with initial
capital letters.

This book is available at quantity discounts for bulk purchases.
For information, please call 1-800-289-0963.

contents

dedicated to Bella and Tucker

I am delighted to donate a percentage of the sales of this book to the International Fund for Animal Welfare (IFAW) and its programs to help pets in the world's poorest communities. IFAW is one of the world's leading animal welfare and conservation organizations. To learn more, please visit *www.ifaw.org*.

acknowledgments

I would like to thank the following people for their support, inspiration, and expertise: Lynn and Ed Rosenfeld; Cynthia and Poptart Rosenfeld; Tara Mark Rosenblum; Tim and Jack Merrill; Amy and Ben Disston; Margo Lyon; Dr. William Carlsen and Staff; Jan Naud; Elizabeth and Diego Ross; June Roberts; Lauren Iungerich; Elizabeth and Gus Sugarman; Joy, Dolly, and Nappy Gorman; Learka and Foxy Bosnak; Janice and Phoenix Roberts; Alyson and Lucia MacInnis; Amanda and Rocky Klein; Laura and LouLou Sfez; Melissa and Kayla Lemer; Felicia and Toluca Wilson; Nancy and Rhett Volpert; Susan, Duke, Kaiser, and Snoopy Jansen; Shirley Jansen; Laura Lee Fulmer; Jascha and Amber Rynek; Daphne and Idaho Zuniga; Elizabeth Oreck; Alexandra Denman and Ben Stein; William Callanan; Maria Cruz; Rita Rivest; Jim Diehl; Cindy Williams; Shelly and Sadie Werner; Lisa and Luigi Rosen; Lewis Fein; Brandan Fouche; Jennifer Fearing; Grace and Daniel Ross; Susan, Hilda and David Rosenfeld; Brownie, Rusty, Byron, Snowy, Chelsea, Foxy, Woody, Ziggy, Tommy, and Trackie Rosenfeld; Nell Copilow; Emily Chan; Jennifer Yousem; Fielding Edlow; Todd Rosenberg; Lucian and Gumbo Piane; Amy and Bernard Stanton; Florence and Bella Lemie; PJ Smith; Dan Schnur; Wendy Liebman; Jeff Sherman; Randee Goldman; Robert Baldwin; Jennifer Kushnier; Andrea Norville; Wendy Simard; Katie Corcoran Lytle; Scott Gould; Jennifer Unter; Smith Long; Rebecca Prange; and Andre Michel Vargas.

introduction

Welcome to *The Complete Single's Guide to Being a Dog Owner*, the ultimate resource for singles raising dogs! In writing this book, I have researched and consulted with experts and everyday dog owners alike to make sure the information you read is accurate and well tested. But most of all, I have drawn upon my own experience raising a particularly amazing Labrador mix named Bella.

Me and Bella

In the fall of 2000, I was working as a producer on the Food Network's hit show **Food 911** *with Tyler Florence. While set-dress shopping for a Chinese-food segment in downtown L.A., I saw a gorgeous black dog darting through traffic. Undeterred by the fact that she was enormous, maybe aggressive, and that I was in the middle of skid row wearing heels, I chased after her for forty-five minutes, until she finally stopped, rolled over, and showed me her belly.*

With her soulful eyes and our deep and immediate attachment, she quickly became Bella Rosenfeld. Eight years and what seems like a lifetime of experience later, Bella takes a daily walk down Rodeo Drive, has lived in four cities, lived through five boyfriends, had three major surgeries, gotten kicked out of day care, and made a valiant-though-failed attempt to swim out to sea. Although I had always been an animal person, nothing prepared me for this stuff! Bella is my inspiration both for **The Complete Single's Guide to Being a Dog Owner** *and my work rescuing dogs. To date, I have personally rescued over 200 dogs and helped thousands more through my work with local Los Angeles-based* *rescues and with IFAW—the International Fund for Animal Welfare (www.ifaw.org).*

While Bella has put me through my paces—providing me with information on how to handle just about any situation—I want to make something abundantly clear from the beginning: If you have questions or concerns about your dog's health, please consult your vet directly. You may be afraid that you're being neurotic and the veterinarian will think you're crazy, but that's okay. Your dog's health must come before your worries about your image.

Speaking of image, names and details in the book have been changed to protect the innocent—and not so innocent—dogs and dog owners I have profiled. So enjoy! And remember, no matter what . . . your dog thinks you rock!

one

considering the commitment

Having Bella has been the most rewarding and gratifying experience of my life. There is simply nothing better than looking into her brown eyes, knowing that she loves me unconditionally and that I am solely responsible for her happiness and well-being. But I wasn't always so sure I was ready for it all. Are you?

Don't worry if you're not. A good way to gauge your puppy potential starts with a simple exercise: Consider the following question.

Why Are You Getting a Dog?

Compare your answers to the following and see which one matches most closely:

A. Dogs are so cute. I have always wanted a [insert your favorite breed].
B. All my friends have dogs and I can't wait to take mine with me everywhere.
C. I've been really stressed and people tell me they think it would be good for me.
D. I am looking forward to caring for a dog and making it a part of my life.

If your answer most resembles A or B, we may have a problem. It's not wrong that you've always wanted to get a Dalmatian and name it Spot, or that your best friend has the most amazing Springer Spaniel so you want one, too. It's just that getting a dog is a major, life-altering decision not to be taken lightly, and not to be made without considering all the responsibilities as well as the rewards. We're not talking about a new pair of shoes, a flat-screen TV, or even a decision to go blonde or shave your head. Dogs are living, breathing creatures that God made cute (especially puppies) for a reason—so that when they destroy those new shoes or keep you up all night there's a better chance that you'll forgive them! But, speaking from experience, the "cute-as-excuse" wears off rapidly, and reality sets in.

If your reason for getting a dog most aligns with C, this could be a problem, too. Countless studies show that the presence of an animal raises people out of depression and lowers stress, but let me be the first to clarify that caring for a dog doesn't make anxiety or stress go away. Truthfully, there are times when dog ownership can add greatly to it.

So the "right" answer to this little quiz is obviously D. Being a single professional who owns a dog comes with all sorts of unexpected challenges, so you had better be excited about making her a big part of your life. Here is a story to illustrate how important it is to want a dog for the right reasons.

Adam and Benji

I recently placed a dog with my friend Adam. He had a high-profile, high-pressure job, and his life was extremely stressful. Worried about his emotional well-being, Adam's family and therapist recommended he get a dog. "It will be a good distraction," they said. For years, Adam had talked about getting a dog, but had never been able to go through with it. He had always wanted a shaggy, Wheaten terrier-type dog, like Benji from the movies, and would often ask if I could find him one. Happy to oblige, I'd send him profiles of available dogs from **www.petfinder.com**, *but he'd inevitably back off, claiming the timing was off. At a certain point, Adam's inquiries became more frequent, so when I came across the perfect Benji-type terrier in a shelter, I called him immediately. Adam had some reservations because of his work schedule, but was elated when he saw the picture and decided that, with my help and a good dog walker, he was ready to adopt his dream dog.*

The dog I found for Adam was an adorable, sweet, eighteen-month-old, potty-trained terrier mix who he named (what else?)

Benji. Like most new dog owners, Adam seemed excited and nervous. He shopped, rearranged his apartment, and read Cesar Millan's **Dog Whisperer** in preparation for his new friend's homecoming, which made me optimistic that he was serious about caring for a dog.

The big day came and, like many dogs coming from the shelter, Benji had a few health problems—nothing too serious, but they were costly. Adam readily stepped up to the plate, paying close to $800 for veterinary care. But, along with his generosity came complaints. Adam reported almost hourly what was going wrong with Benji. "He has diarrhea, he ate some computer paper, he cries when I leave him alone, etc." The first forty-eight hours with any dog are bound to be rough, so I figured things would get better. And they did . . . for a while.

Adam eventually called less frequently as he and Benji adjusted to one another—but soon the complaints started again, this time with a new angle. He loved Benji, but he spoke of the many "sacrifices" he was making. "It really stresses me out to think of him alone after day care. I still want to have a life, you know? How am I going to find a girlfriend? Do you think it's imperative that I come straight home at night after work?" He lamented how much money he had to spend on the dog. I recommended trainers and even offered to find another home for Benji, but he said he really did love him, and would make it work, but just needed to vent.

Meanwhile, Benji felt Adam's frustration and his actions reflected it. Although a stellar canine at doggy day care, Benji's behavior deteriorated while at home: He nipped at people and peed in the house. It was a terrible cycle. Adam got stressed, Benji acted out, which in turn made Adam more stressed, and so on, until Adam resented Benji and, sadly, Benji feared Adam.

I'm always asked why there are so many dogs in shelters. Unfortunately, Benji's story is a common one for dogs who end up in the pound. Adam wasn't a bad person and Benji wasn't a bad dog; Adam just didn't understand what having a dog entailed. He wanted the benefits of having a dog—the companionship, the unconditional love—and figured a dog would just slip into his single, career-driven lifestyle without him having to make adjustments to his work schedule or social calendar. Because I wanted Adam to have a dog and I had been able to make changes when I got Bella, I assumed he would be able to do the same. It's something I'll never do again, because dogs don't simply slip into your lifestyle—especially if you're single. Unless you get very lucky with a younger dog or you adopt an older dog, you are going to have to adapt your lifestyle to accommodate theirs.

Thankfully, I was able to find a new home for Benji, and now he is extremely happy. The key difference between Adam and Benji's new owner is that, while the new owner has an equally demanding job, he was willing to adjust his lifestyle to accommodate his dog, welcoming Benji and his needs with open arms. Benji has not had one accident in the house or nipped at a single person since the move.

CANINE CONSIDERATION ❖ ❖ ❖

Take your lifestyle into consideration when deciding whether or not you should get a dog. If you're not willing to adjust your schedule to accommodate his, you may not be ready.

considering the commitment

Disclaimer

This section, like this entire book, is not meant to discourage you from getting a dog. In fact, quite the opposite—I want to empower people by offering practical information on what it takes to be a dog owner. Remember, you alone are going to be this animal's primary caregiver. So, if you can't live up to the demands of caring for a dog, or you don't want to, you will likely end up with an unhappy puppy on your hands.

Remember: Dogs can't speak or rationally discuss their frustrations, so they communicate in other ways—like peeing in your bed, eating their poop, or opting for your favorite shoes as their chew-toy du jour. So for the sake of the dog, your carpet, and your sanity, be sure you're ready to commit to your new pet.

Are You Ready for the Commitment of Having a Dog?

When you responsibly contemplate having a dog, the enormity of it all can be overwhelming. While later chapters will cover many of these topics in greater detail, here is a general overview of what to expect, organized by commitments: time commitment, financial commitment, and emotional commitment.

Time Commitment

Dogs require an enormous time commitment on your part— today, tomorrow, and, if all goes well, for years to come. The following gives you a basic idea of the nature of this time commitment and some ideas about how you as a young, single person can work a dog into your busy schedule.

▼ Daily Commitment

Dogs are social creatures. They will not be happy if left alone for too long (remember, an unhappy dog can be a destructive dog). So, in order to achieve a successful balance between your needs and your dog's, be ready to commit at least an hour a day to your four-legged friend. You can break up this hour throughout the day as you wish. Depending on your schedule and your pooch's potty needs (some dogs can't hold it for more than four hours, others can hold it for up to eight), maybe it's twenty or thirty minutes of attention in the morning with the remaining time spent either with a midday walk or one in the evening with a before-bed bathroom break. The morning block includes the basics—food, water, and a chance to do her business, as well as an opportunity for her to burn up some energy so she doesn't eat your couch while you're at work. The afternoon or evening block must also include a chance for your dog to get outside, stretch her legs, go potty, and, of course, eat supper.

The kind of activity can vary based on your dog and your lifestyle. Maybe you play with your dog in a yard or at a park, take a run or a walk, or work on manners and reinforce training. You can adjust the blocks to fit your schedule and that of your dog; everyone's schedule is going to be different. Maybe you work near home. Maybe you like to work out in the morning. Maybe you hire a dog walker to do one of the blocks. There are infinite possibilities.

If the prospect of this sort of time commitment stresses you out, ask your friends who own dogs how they do it. Everyone figures it out in a different way and has different challenges. Some dogs need more frequent potty breaks (puppies need to go at least every two to three hours) and some dogs need longer periods of exercise. Maybe you have neighbors or friends nearby with dogs who you could talk to about setting up a playgroup or about sharing walking duties. This works out really well if you trust both them and their dog.

The kind of exercise/attention you choose to do with/give your dog can vary day to day and dog to dog. For older dogs, a simple walk around the block and a brushing might be enough for a morning, then a walk and short game of fetch in the afternoon. Younger dogs, puppies, and certain breeds require much more than sixty minutes. But no matter what kind of dog you have, regardless of size or age, there is something that goes for every owner: You are your dog's lifeline. It doesn't matter if it's snowing outside, you throw your back out, or you have a date—your dog needs you and you must be

DOGMA:

Doing Your Duty!

As an owner, it's your responsibility to clean up any "presents" your dog leaves behind. However, it's easy to forget to bring a poop bag each time you walk your dog. To avoid being caught bagless, I have "Bags on Board" dispensers attached to all of my leashes. This genius little contraption holds a roll of fifteen biodegradable doggie clean-up bags. Remembering to restock once every fifteen times is a lot easier than remembering to grab a bag every time you walk out the door!

willing to care for him during these and other inconvenient times. This is the commitment you made when you got a dog. Resenting this commitment is a recipe for disaster—remember Adam?

CANINE CONSIDERATION ❖ ❖ ❖

Commit to spending at least an hour a day caring for your dog. Make it 15/15/30 or 20/20/20; any combination of the sixty minutes should work for most adult dogs. Any less, though, and you're asking for trouble.

▼ Weekly Commitment

For most working singles, fitting sixty minutes into a workday to care for a dog can be challenging. It's not a good thing if you are continually unable to fit this time in to care for your dog, but we all have crazy weeks sometimes, and that's okay! So if you're not quite reaching the quality sixty-minute mark, make up for it with more quality time on the weekends. Stay longer at the park. Take longer and more frequent walks. If weather permits and your dog enjoys it, go for a swim.

Be sure your dog's stamina can keep up with the excitement she has about a weekend activity. If she's not fit enough or used to an activity she, like people, can overheat and become ill. Due to the way they breathe, some dogs like Pugs, French and English Bulldogs, and Pekingese are especially prone to these problems.

Another weekly activity, especially for longhaired dogs such as Poodles, Terriers, Spaniels, Australian Shepherds, and Newfoundlands, is to give them a good brushing. Most dogs will love it and it keeps their coat shiny, as well as keeping the stink factor down between washings.

▼ Monthly Commitment

Monthly responsibilities for your dog are small, but important. As it's best to keep your dog's food fresh, I recommend buying food monthly or every six weeks. It's best to feed your dog human-grade or preservative-free dog food, which is not usually available at chain supermarkets or grocery stores. You will have to make a special visit to your neighborhood pet store or order it online.

Another monthly chore is grooming and preventative medicine application. Bella gets washed monthly or bimonthly depending on the season, and on the first Sunday of every month I apply flea-control medication. In some areas of the country where heartworm is an issue, you will also have to administer heartworm medication on a monthly basis.

▼ Yearly Commitment

In order to keep your dog healthy, you must provide him with consistent medical care and vaccinations by getting him a yearly checkup. Your vet should send out reminders for you to bring in your dog, but if they forget or you don't have a regular vet, take the initiative to find a vet and schedule a checkup.

CANINE CONSIDERATION ❖ ❖ ❖

Bring your dog in for a yearly checkup (even if you don't go in for one yourself)!

▼ Lifetime Commitment

Dogs aren't a passing fancy. They are a long-term commitment. If you get a puppy and you're lucky, this could mean fifteen years or longer. Even if you get an older dog, you are still committing to a longer relationship than many people have ever had with a significant other. Realize also that having a dog will impact all aspects of your future. You'll have to consider things like whether you'll be moving to a new house or maybe a new state. If so, you will need to find a dog-friendly apartment, which can take more time to find and may cost more money per month. What will you do if you find an amazing partner who happens to hate dogs? Are you planning on having kids? Two common reasons people give up dogs are that they either get involved with someone who doesn't like dogs or have kids and don't want the responsibility of caring for both a dog and a baby.

CANINE CONSIDERATION ❖ ❖ ❖

You can't predict the future, but realize when you decide to get a dog you must be willing to make some extra effort when life changes inevitably come around.

If this discussion of time commitment seems overwhelming, here is a chart to help you plan for the time involved in caring for your dog.

		TIME COMMITMENT		
Frequency	Daily	Weekly	Monthly	Yearly
Food	Twice daily		Buy food	
Attention	60 minutes minimum	Big trip to the park or extra long walk		
Vet/Meds	Pills if needed		Flea prevention/Heartworm meds	Yearly checkup
Grooming		Brushing	Trip to the groomers	

Financial Commitment

The financial commitment of dog ownership goes way beyond your initial costs. Regardless of where you get your pet, there will be ongoing costs that vary by breed and size. The rule of thumb is the bigger the dog the higher the cost for food, grooming, and medical care. Teacup dogs are an exception. Due to their extremely small size and questionable breeding background, they tend to have serious health issues, resulting in higher vet costs.

To help you budget, here is an overview of how dog ownership affects your wallet:

▼ Food

Your food costs will vary depending on your dog's size and the quality of the food you buy. The smaller the dog the lower your food costs will be. However, when it comes to food, don't be fooled by the cost per bag; all food is not created equal. Higher-quality food may be pricier, but it is nutritionally dense, so dogs eat less of it. The cost of feeding your dog better food is less than feeding her cheap food.

In addition, better-quality food will save you money because dogs, like people, are what they eat. By choosing to feed your dog cheap food to save money, you will ultimately pay later with higher vet bills since highly processed, lower-quality foods can cause your dog to suffer conditions such as skin allergies, early onset arthritis, or even cancer.

CANINE CONSIDERATION ❖ ❖ ❖

To properly feed most dogs, expect to pay between $25 and $45 a month for food and basic treats. For large dogs like Mastiffs and Saint Bernards, expect to pay around $60 per month.

▼ Vet and Pet Insurance

It is impossible to anticipate what your vet costs will be per year. Dogs that are healthy and only require a yearly checkup and vaccinations will cost anywhere from $150 to $250 per year, depending on your city and your dog's age. Puppies cost more because of required immunizations and the fee for spay/neuter surgery, which can run anywhere between $100 and $500 depending on your dog's size. Older dogs may also cost more due to common disease screenings that require blood tests or X-rays.

Unfortunately, few dogs live an accident- or illness-free life. It is impossible to anticipate every possible scenario. Bella woke up one day, couldn't walk straight, didn't want to eat—unusual for her—and had white gums. It turned out that her spleen had burst for no obvious reason and she was bleeding internally. The surgery cost $2,300 but, thankfully, my pet insurance covered 70 percent of that bill. Pet insurance pays your veterinary costs if your dog is ill or has an accident. Some policies also pay out if the pet dies, is lost, or is stolen. Pet insurance premiums vary depending on level of coverage, from around $10 a month for accident-only coverage to $60+ for more complete coverage, including illness and even boarding costs. There is an additional premium for certain breeds like Soft Coated Wheaten Terriers, French Bulldogs, and others because unlike mutts (who are the healthiest dogs) and other less-sensitive purebreds, these breeds are more prone to expensive illnesses. Policies usually offer to pay a certain percentage of vet costs minus a $50–$100 deductible depending on the company.

CANINE CONSIDERATION ❖ ❖ ❖

Save money—protect your pet. Get pet insurance. Good vet care, like good human healthcare, isn't always cheap. I love my vet, and while he's not cheap, having pet insurance for Bella allows me to give her the best care possible.

▼ License and Microchip

Many jurisdictions require you to license your dog. Although getting licensed may seem like a hassle, the license tag on your dog's collar tells anyone who sees her that she belongs to someone. Dog licenses usually feature a distinct number so if a dog is found, an owner's information is on file and they can be located.

Pet licensing also helps curb outbreaks of animal illness by requiring owners to inoculate their pets in order to get the license. License fees range by city, from about $10 to $25 for fixed animals to sometimes over $100 for unfixed animals. Cities charge more for a dog that's not fixed as a way to increase spaying and neutering, the only way to stabilize pet overpopulation.

Another way to protect dogs is to have them microchipped. Programmable chips, about the size of a grain of rice, are injected under the skin on a dog's neck. When a pet comes into a shelter or is found and brought to a vet, the shelter staff will use a scanner to read the information embedded in the chip and can then find the dog's owner. Often, the first thing that happens when a dog gets out is his tag or collar falls off. A microchip becomes the only hope an owner has of finding his or her dog. Dogs can also run miles in a day and some dogs are stolen only to be dumped in another town. Owners don't always know which animal-control facilities to check to find them, but microchips—at a cost of about $40, including registration and the procedure to insert—allow a dog to be linked back to its owner no matter how far away he gets.

CANINE CONSIDERATION ❖ ❖ ❖

Get your dog licensed and microchipped. It's worth the cost.

▼ Grooming

Grooming is a cost you may not have thought about when planning for a dog. However, it is essential for both your sanity—who wants a smelly dog?—as well as your dog's health. Just like people, a dog's physical state can impact her sense of well-being. There are extreme cases of neglected dogs with matted and dirty coats who, once cleaned, demonstrated exuberance and joy. Of course, you won't let your precious pooch get to such a state, but letting her hair get matted or her fur too greasy or dirty can still negatively impact her mood.

Different dogs require different kinds of grooming at different price points. Hair dogs like Maltese, Bichons, Poodles, and Shi Tzus need regular grooming including hair trimming, brush-outs, and the removal of tear stains around their eyes. Depending on where you live, a grooming can cost anywhere from $25 to $85. Fur dogs like Golden Retrievers, Boxers, and Bulldogs also need to be groomed, but their grooming is usually limited to a bath and maybe a body shave to keep them cool. An average bath for a fur dog should cost between $25 and $65, depending on the size of your dog, and you can expect to pay about the same for a shave.

As a loving and financially astute owner the prospect of $25–$85 a month, or even every two months, may inspire you to bathe your dog at home. Unfortunately, grooming your dog yourself isn't the best idea, especially for hair dogs like Poodles or Maltese. Like human hair, each dog has a different texture that requires different treatment—i.e., your hairdresser will cut curly thick hair differently than she will straight fine hair. A professional groomer will be familiar with the differences between dogs' coats and be able to give your dog the appropriate trim.

Although grooming a fur dog at home certainly requires less skill, you still have to know what you're doing. Are you using the right shampoo for your dog's coat? Are you able to fully dry your dog before going outside if it's cold? Are you getting all the shampoo out of his coat? A professional grooming takes the guesswork out of grooming your dog and can offer key benefits: Your bathtub stays clean; the groomer trims your dog's nails (something you have to be careful about doing yourself); cleans his ears; and, most importantly, expresses his anal glands—something that you definitely want to avoid taking on by yourself.

Anal glands contain a pungent fluid that ancestral wild dogs and wolves would strategically release to mark their territory. Today's domesticated dogs no longer have the same need for or control of these glands and the fluid can back up. The backup, known as having "impacted" anal glands, at best leads to a stinky tush; at worst, it can cause a painful and even dangerous infection. Thus, your dog needs you or your groomer to "express" or drain the fluid from her glands on her behalf. Expressing anal glands is not a pleasant job, nor is it one for the uninitiated. I highly recommend forking over the extra cash to get your dog professionally groomed somewhere so-called "anals" are part of the grooming service.

CANINE CONSIDERATION ❖ ❖ ❖

Find a good groomer, and plan to have your dog professionally groomed monthly or bimonthly. To save money, brush your dog's coat between grooming appointments, which removes dirt and loose hair and keeps her coat shiny and clean.

▼ Training

Providing adequate training for your dog is a fundamental part of being a good owner. There are many different kinds of training, ranging from the basic "sit, stay, and heel" to agility training to behavioral modification training for those dogs that have developed unwanted behaviors. Similarly, there are numerous ways to train your dog, ranging from following a book or DVD program to taking basic obedience classes to working with a private trainer.

Start with the essentials when estimating the cost of training a dog. If you get a puppy or even a grown dog, it is important to begin with a dog and puppy class. They may seem basic, but are crucial. Group classes not only teach you and your dog the basics (sit, stay, come), but provide an opportunity for him to socialize with other dogs and to get comfortable with you as his owner. Classes usually run for four to six weeks, one day a week, and cost between $100 and $200. If your dog displays any additional behavior problems—such as enduring separation anxiety, problems with potty training, fear, or aggression—consult a trainer. These issues can often pass with just a little guidance coupled with your commitment to following the trainer's advice.

A session with a good trainer in your home can cost between $75 and $250 per session. This is an important investment, the dividends of which will pay off for a lifetime.

When looking for a trainer, cost does not mean quality. Ask your vet, ask a friend you trust, call your breeder, or ask the local dog rescue for a good referral. Also, be sure you feel comfortable with your trainer and that they understand your goals and the realities of your lifestyle.

▼ Necessities

When getting a dog, certain purchases are necessary. Based on my experience accompanying new owners on their first trips to the pet supply store, it's easy to spend upwards of $300 getting set up. It is so easy to go off the deep end with all the fun new things available, but try to control yourself. Stick to what you really need in the first few days. PETCO, Target, and PetSmart will all still be there tomorrow, so start with the necessities:

- **Food:** (get a small bag and ask for samples of other kinds of food because your dog might not like the food you choose) $15
- **Treats:** (get a small bag) $10

- **Crate/Baby Gate:** $50–$150
- **Collar and leash:** $15–Unlimited
- **Toys:** $5–$20
- **Wee-Wee pads** (for puppies and un-housetrained dogs) $25
- **Nature's Miracle:** (for cleaning) $8
- **Flea control:** $12–$16
- **Dog bed:** $20–$200
- **Water and food bowls:** (or use bowls from home until you can get the fancy bowls you have your eye on) $10–$50

Even for the essentials, costs add up quickly. On the low end, the list above comes close to $200! So, do some research and look for any and all available coupons. Also, many smaller pet stores offer a first-time discount if you adopt a dog and are bringing it in for its first shopping spree! Scan craigslist.org and garage sales for used crates and baby gates. These are expensive items when purchased new, but can often be found in good shape secondhand for a fraction of the cost.

CANINE CONSIDERATION ❖ ❖ ❖

There are many financial issues to consider when getting a dog, so go to the store with a budget in mind and stick to the necessities.

All of these costs swirling around in your head can be intimidating. Use the matrix of costs on the following page as a guide. And if you don't have the funds for a new dog crate and have to get a used one or you can only afford to get your dog professionally groomed every three months instead of two, that's okay. But if costs for the vet and vaccinations are beyond your financial capability, do the right thing and wait until you have the available funds. In the meantime, foster a dog for a local humane society, pet sit for a friend, or start saving for your doggie trust fund. Don't worry! It will only be a matter of time before you'll be able to afford the dog of your dreams.

PET OWNERSHIP COSTS				
Frequency	**Day 1**	**Monthly**	**Occasional**	**Yearly**
Food	$20–$60	$20–$60 depending on size of dog		$240–$720
Treats	$10	$10		$120
Vet— including vaccines and spay/ neuter	$150–$600: includes spay/neuter, vet to check out your dog, and vaccines		$150–$400: for unavoid-able accidents, illnesses, and vaccines	Year 1=$300–$1,000, Year 2 and beyond=$150–$400
Preventa-tive Meds		$12–$16 per month for flea and tick; $5–$10 per month for heartworm		$200–$320
Training	$100–$200 for group puppy classes; $300–$1,000 for private training		$75–$150 Refresher with trainer	Year 1=$100–$1,000; Year 2=$0–$150
Grooming	$25–$60	$25–$60 (Varies by dog; some only need every 2 months)		$150–$720

Frequency	Day 1	Monthly	Occasional	Yearly
License and Micro-chipping	$10–$50			$10–$50
Boarding (assuming a 1-week vacation)			$150–$350	$150–$350
Crate	$50–$150			Year 1=$50–$150; Year 2 & Beyond= $0–$150
Insurance	$10–$50	$10–$50/per month depending on coverage level		$120–$600
Necessities	$150–$350		$75–$250 for upgrades and when your dog grows	Year 1=$50–$425; Year 2 and beyond= $75–$250
Totals	$525–$1,530	$82–$206	$450–$1,150	$1,450–$5,500

▼ Emotional Commitment

Finally, there is the issue of the emotional commitment a person must make to have a dog. Being an owner demands as much of an emotional commitment as it does a pledge of money or time. Dogs are highly sensitive and intuitive creatures and, as with Adam and Benji, if you resent having the responsibility of having a dog you may not have the best experience as an owner. Getting Bella forced me to grow in ways I didn't know I could or even needed to. Forget having to clean up her poop or learning how to get muddy paw prints out of a carpet. I had to learn to forgive her when she did things like puke all over my oriental rug or when she knocked over and broke an antique vase with a wag of her tail. Dogs are dogs. They don't understand words. However, they do connect to tone and emotion. Of course you can get upset (within reason) when training a dog (they just peed on the floor or they pulled on the leash), but if you get upset and your dog can't connect it to a particular behavior, you will just make her confused and nervous rather than encouraging her not to repeat her mistake.

I had to learn to be patient and realize that, in my relationship with Bella, I was no longer a kid; I was the one in charge and needed to act accordingly because a dog looks to its master—its alpha—for guidance. Whether or not you can take care of yourself, you have to be able to take care of your dog's needs. This means stepping up to the plate, fulfilling the time commitments and the financial commitments, and being in charge. Otherwise, you'll have a nervous and unhappy dog on your hands.

So take your dog to the vet every year, walk her even if it's cold outside, and don't get upset with her if she ___ (fill in the blank). In return for your commitment, your dog will give back to you a million times over with her undying affection and love.

So now that you know what to expect, how do you know if you're ready? How will you be able to handle a life where vet visits, vomit, and vaccinations are as important as playing, puppyhood, and park trips when you haven't been to the doctor in years and regularly forget to pay your electric bill? Don't worry; you can still be a great owner. I've seen people rise spectacularly to the occasion, surprising themselves and everyone around them with how well they can care for another creature when they are failures at taking care of themselves. The truth is, for the love of a dog you can do more than you ever thought possible, but remember, this is a huge responsibility and you should only make the commitment if you really want to.

the best breeds for single living

Just like Adam who had always wanted a Benji-esque dog or my sister Cynthia who dreamed of having a Dalmatian, owners-to-be usually have a breed or type of dog in mind. Whether this is because Jessica Simpson's maltipoo is cute or your neighbors growing up had a Golden Retriever, these are not compelling reasons to choose one particular breed over another. A smart owner-to-be will move beyond the superficial and, instead, decide which breed is a good match for their lifestyle. Choosing a dog is like Internet dating. You wouldn't (or shouldn't) sign on to Match.com and pick a date based on pictures alone, and you shouldn't pick a dog this way, either.

When selecting a dog, you're committing to that dog for its lifetime, not just suffering through one bad date; so, choosing a dog based on what it looks like or even what size it is can get you into big trouble. Personality is everything, and all dogs are different. Remember, breeds will behave differently based on what that particular breed was created to do.

What's in a Breed?

Descended from domesticated wolves, modern dog breeds were developed by selecting dogs with specific characteristics and mating their descendants until the chosen characteristics—size, mental capacity, hunting instinct—became primary. Most breeds were, in fact, developed to perform a specific job such as herding, hunting, guarding, or even to be a comforting companion.

In purebreds, instinct and behavior have been bred out in favor of coat and conformation, and mixed out in the case of mutts, but purebreds or mixes that have one dominant breed in their mix will, for the most part, tend to behave in certain ways that are deeply set in their DNA. Fighting a dog's instinct can be an uphill battle. So choosing a dog for looks instead of what he is predisposed to be like could be a disaster.

It's important to figure out what qualities you're looking for in a pup to avoid this type of upheaval. You don't want to bring home a dog that sheds heavily if you have problems with allergies and you don't want to buy a breed that requires a lot of attention if you work late at the office six days a week. To avoid adopting a pooch that doesn't fit with your lifestyle, the key is research, research, and more research. Check out the different inherited qualities of any breed that you're considering adopting and weigh them against your expectations.

To find out which breed may work for you, check out the dog compatibility tests available through *http://animal.discovery.com /breedselector/dogselectorindex.do,* found on the Animal Planet's website. The tests allow owners-to-be to answer a series of questions and then match them up with the breeds that are best suited for their lifestyle. Similarly, it's nice to have a comparison of breeds on the issues singles care about. Here's a quick reference list that focuses on the top ten breeds as listed by the AKC and how they match up to some important single-owner considerations.

DOGMA:

Make Mine a Mutt

While this chart is limited to breeds, I do not mean to imply that you should only consider getting a purebred. Mutts are the best dogs you can have, both in terms of health and temperament. So really, the greatest thing a single owner-to-be can do is peruse the list and see what breed suits her best, do a little more research online and in books, and then find a mutt with that dominant breed.

	Shedding*	Energy Level	Tendency for Barking
Retrievers (Labrador)	Moderate to high	High (as pups) to moderate (as adults)	Moderate
Yorkshire Terriers	Low	High	High
German Shepherds	High	High (as pups) to moderate (as adults)	High
Retrievers (Golden)	High	High (as pups) to moderate (as adults)	Moderate
Beagles	Moderate	Moderate	High
Boxers	Moderate to low	High	Medium
Dachshunds	Low to moderate	High	High
Poodles	Low	Moderate to high	Moderate to high
Shih Tzus	Low	Moderate	Moderate
Bulldogs	Moderate	Low	Low

Lifespan	Independence	Weight in Pounds
10–12	Needy	55–80+
14–16	Needy	< 7
10–12	Needy	75–95+
10–13	Needy	55–75+
12–15	Moderately independent	18–30
8–10	Needy	50–80
12–14	Moderately needy	8–28 (< 11 is a min. and >11 is a standard)
12–15	Needy	4–65 (4–8 Toy; 12–18 Miniature; 45–65 Standard)
11–14	Moderately needy	9–16
8–12	Needy	40–55

*Remember, as a dog's shedding level goes down, its grooming demands often go up. Dogs such as Poodles and Shih Tzus have a coat that must be brushed frequently to avoid matting.

the best breeds for single living

If none of the above breeds meets your ideal, consider a breed that you may not have thought of. Singles who want . . .

A quiet dog:
should consider a Basenji because they don't bark

A low-shed, large dog:
should consider a Giant Schnauzer because they are big and powerful, but have the same low-shed coat as their miniature and standard counterparts

A low-shed, medium dog:
should consider a Bedlington Terrier because they have a playful disposition and shed very little

A low-shed, small dog:
should consider a West Highland Terrier because they have a low-shed, low allergy-inducing coat and are easy to train

A lower-energy dog:
should consider a Greyhound because they're great sprinters, but also love to chill on the couch

An independent dog:
should consider a Chow Chow or a Shar Pei because they are reserved and self-possessed

A healthy dog:
should consider a mutt because the diversity of their genetic makeup makes them less susceptible to ailments common in purebred dogs

A dog you don't have to take care of:
should consider a stuffed animal because all dogs need love and attention

This is not a complete list by any means; I simply couldn't include all the wonderful breeds out there. The AKC recognizes over 150 breeds, and then there are the numerous hybrid dogs out there, all the Poos, Moodles, and Doodles . . . even Schnoodles and Labradoodles! To research more breeds recognized by the AKC, take a look at the extensive chart in Appendix B.

A note while we're on the topic: Designer dogs are extremely popular and interest many people because of the low-shed factor. Unfortunately, there is a great deal of inbreeding with these dogs, and you would be *much* better off finding a mixed-breed Schnauzer, Wheaten Terrier, or naturally occurring Poo-ish or Doodle-ish dog in a shelter or rescue group. These dogs will be far healthier and similarly low shedding.

Many of the breeds listed may not be ones you would think of as being a good fit for a single person, or may be breeds you hadn't thought of at all. But keep an open mind; there is not a singular all-dog personality.

Not all dogs of a particular breed will behave exactly the same. Genetics, how a dog was raised, its pack position in its litter as a puppy, and a whole host of other things can impact a dog's personality. I know Basset Hounds who bite and Pit Bulls who work as therapy dogs. There are both exceptions to breed tendencies as well as many inaccurate stereotypes to look out for. Pit Bulls are often very sweet, gentle dogs who are well suited for apartment life, while Jack Russell Terriers, although small and cute, are not so great for apartments due to their outsized need for exercise and mental stimulation.

Breeds provide a good frame of reference for finding the right dog for your lifestyle. However, do your homework and don't trust stereotypes.

Despite knowing the sometimes less-than-charming behavioral tendencies of popular breeds and what kind of dog would be best suited to your lifestyle it's still easy to fall in love with the look of a certain breed. Be careful not to get fixated on a dog's looks instead of its behavior. Being wooed by a dog's inherent cuteness or because you have some idea in your head of what your perfect dog is supposed to look like can be a very, very bad thing. Trust me; I speak from experience.

Meet Brownie

My parents agreed to get a third dog just after my sister Cynthia's dog, Poptart, spent a winter at their house. When Cynthia took Poptart back to New York for the spring, my parents' dog, Rusty, fell apart. He lost weight, started peeing in the house, and even began to lose some of his coat. After a trip to the vet, who ruled out illness, we consulted a trainer who explained that Rusty simply missed Poptart. The trainer suggested getting another dog, a prospect I was elated at and my mother hesitantly accepted.

Turning to my rescue friends, I looked at the dogs they had in rescue and immediately saw the adorable face of Brownie, a three-year-old Yorkshire Terrier. My heart melted and I had to adopt him. Because of my relationship with the group and the fact that rescuers love to stay in touch with the dogs they place, I got to the head of the line and took him to my parents.

As I was leaving the sanctuary with Brownie, the head of the group, June, kept asking me, "Are you sure you really want this dog?" I should have picked up on her hesitation, but like many owners-to-be, I was obsessed with Brownie's incurable cuteness. I had not yet learned the dangers of choosing looks over personality.

Brownie exceeds the weight and height specifications for Yorkies according to the American Kennel Club, but his behavior is right on target for a Yorkshire Terrier—something I should have paid closer attention to before I brought him home to my parents. The Elite Pets Internet Club gives what I think is the ultimate description of what I now know to be the true Yorkie personality: "Yorkshire Terriers are alert, vivacious, playful, charming, and clever. They don't need a lot of exercise but do like to run and play. Despite its little

DOGMA:

Keep in Touch

When adopting, keep the rescuer or rescue group posted on your dog's progress. Good news keeps morale high and inspires rescuers to continue doing their work. However, if you're having ongoing problems, ask your rescuer for help. Be nice about it and don't threaten to bring the dog back; simply ask for guidance. Most rescuers have been around the block a few times and can be a valuable resource for information.

size, the Yorkie is fearless, saucy, and always eager for challenges. They defend their territory and are excellent watchdogs."

All things considered, my family loves Brownie to pieces, but he is certainly not the type of dog my mother had originally agreed to adopt. "Fearless, saucy, and always eager for challenges" turned out to mean unendingly energetic, which Brownie shows by rifling through the garbage, humping things (preferably my mother's down pillows), and protecting the house from invasion by threats such as the mailman, passing cars, and air. He is indeed up for any challenge, as long as it's not the challenge of becoming potty trained, a skill that Yorkies are notorious for having difficulty acquiring. Even with their quirks, Yorkies are the second most-popular breed in America (Labradors are first) and the undisputed "it dog" of choice for celebutantes worldwide, but they are first and foremost terriers with a terrier attitude.

DOGMA:

Dog in Distress!

Watch your dog's reactions to situational changes such as adding or losing a dog, moving, even breaking up with a boyfriend. Dogs commonly show their anxiety or distress through weight loss, loss of hair, peeing or pooping in the house when they were previously potty trained, and sometimes showing new negative behaviors such as nipping or growling. If you notice these behaviors it's best to consult your vet or a trusted trainer.

Behavioral issues aside, my parents adore Brownie and won't be giving him up anytime soon. They have a yard, someone home all day, and dual incomes to replace items such as the $100 bill he ate. However, for a single professional starting out in the world, ending up with a misbehaved dog like Brownie could pose a problem.

Elizabeth and Gus

Formerly single, now married dog-owner Elizabeth has a Yorkie named Gus whose terrible terrier behavior almost got her kicked out of her apartment building. Apparently, Gus didn't like the Cocker Spaniel living in the apartment below them. Staying true to his innate need to defend his territory, Gus would go ballistic every time they passed the Cocker's front or back door. It was bad. I live across the street from her and I knew her exact comings and goings by the sound of Gus's shrieks.

Neighbors complained to the building management, and it became quite the ordeal. Elizabeth had great patience with Gus and tried working through the situation with a trainer, but she finally got lucky when the neighbors unexpectedly moved out. Of course, not everyone has such patience—or such luck. This, again, is why so many dogs end up in rescue or in the shelter. Elizabeth doesn't regret having gotten a Yorkie now; she loves Gus more than anything, but would she recommend a Yorkie to her single friends? Not necessarily. That is, unless that friend found either an older Yorkie to adopt or was willing to do a LOT of training with the Yorkie from day one. The good news is that Gus did mellow out; maybe that means there is still hope for our Brownie.

If you don't think you'd be able to deal with a dog like Brownie, don't worry. That doesn't mean you'd be a bad dog owner or that you're unloving; it just means you need to pick a dog that's better suited to your single lifestyle. For example, one that won't freak out if you live in an apartment, when you go to work, or when you, hopefully, go out on dates.

In many cases, better suited really means a more independent dog, which is a trait of Shiba Inus, Basenjis, Shar-Peis, and Chows. It's not that these dogs don't need people—all dogs need people, they are social animals—but these breeds tend to be more aloof than, say, a Maltese, who will cry if it's not being held. One caveat, though: The flipside of a dog's independence is often some personal space issues, meaning the dog might not be friendly to everyone—especially children. This may be fine for now, but remember, you might not be a single (childless) owner forever. So, to avoid having to give up a beloved dog in the future, choose your dog wisely and for the long haul.

DOGMA:

Decisions, Decisions

Having a dog can be such an amazing and yet challenging experience. Don't make things harder for yourself by getting a dog that doesn't fit your lifestyle because there are so many dogs that will.

Decide What You Do and Don't Want in a Dog

Shelly is the ultimate hip, single New Yorker. We met in a book club when we both lived in Seattle, and Shelly quickly became one of Bella's favorites. Shelly moved around a lot, but once she got to NYC, she felt at home and ready to get a dog.

Being the in-the-know person that she is, Shelly consciously made a "mutt map" and figured out what she was looking for in a small breed that would fit her lifestyle. She knew whatever dog she picked would be cute, so she concentrated on the behavioral attributes and personal characteristics her perfect dog would have. It would be a nonyappy companion with moderate exercise requirements who was sweet, lower-shedding, able to travel (fitting under the seat when she traveled home to Seattle), and would possess some personality traits of a sight dog or hunting dog—essentially a big dog in a little dog's body.

Shelly researched breeds for about a year. Using the Internet and breed books, she compared her mutt map against the descriptions of various smaller-breed dogs. From her research, a Cavalier King Charles fit Shelly's needs perfectly. The *Encyclopedia of Dog Breeds* (a great reference!) goes so far as to say, "The Cavalier in many ways fits the bill as an ideal house pet. It is sweet, gentle, playful, willing to please, affectionate, and quiet. It is amiable towards other dogs, pets, and strangers." Indeed, Cavs were a perfect match for Shelly in the city; all she had to do was find one.

CANINE CONSIDERATION ❖ ❖ ❖

Make a mutt map. Think about what your ideal dog will be like. There are no right or wrong answers; that's the genius thing! No matter what you're looking for, if you keep your options open, you'll find there is a wide range of dogs to fit your lifestyle.

Canine Characteristics to Consider

1. **Coat**—Be realistic about your willingness to clean up loose hair, give regular brushings, and or take your dog to the salon for regular grooming. If you choose none of the above, you may want to reconsider getting a dog.

2. **Exercise**—Are you willing to take your dog to the dog park and let her play come rain or come shine? Are you a runner who wants a companion so you can run trails after work? Or maybe you're kind of a couch potato and want to have a dog that doesn't need a ton of exercise?

3. **Size**—How big or small do you need to go? Do you travel and need a dog to fit under the seat? Or maybe you're a renter; picking a smaller dog may be a requirement for these reasons. However, focusing on size can be misleading. Many small dogs need yards to run around in, while an English Mastiff—who won't be getting past any condo boards for being under twenty pounds—requires only daily leash walks and the occasional extended park play.

4. **Health**—Not all dogs are equally healthy. Due to genetic diversity, meaning a reduced chance of hereditary diseases, mutts are predisposed to be healthier than purebreds. Certain purebred breeds—either because of a long history of interbreeding or because of their sensitive makeup—will often end up with higher veterinary bills. Popular breeds such as French Bulldogs, Italian Greyhounds, Bernese Mountain Dogs, and Soft Coated Wheaten Terriers, among others, will cost more to insure due to their statistical predisposition to illness and or accidents. The Chinese Shar-Pei is so prone to illness that some carriers will only cover them for accidents.

5. **Mellow factor**—A dog's ability and, really, their proclivity to be mellow is a particularly important trait for singles to look for when choosing a dog. As a single person, you probably aren't home much during the day, want to have a social life, and don't want to replace your personal belongings on a regular basis. Yet, so often a dog's current mellowness or even their future aptitude for it is overlooked during the selection process. Instead, singles tend to think of the dogs they know who belong to family or friends, often forgetting that these dogs aren't puppies anymore and have already been through the worst phases of destructive high-energy behavior.

Want a Mellow Dog? Get an Older Dog

When deciding what dog to get, so many people automatically think of getting a puppy. Unfortunately, even the best dogs you know were absolute terrors as puppies and, moreover, there isn't anything fun about having to get up in the middle of the night to clean up puppy poop or replace shoes and furniture. And, unlike life with your childhood dog, your mom isn't around to clean up. It's all on you. So please consider the following mantra when picking your dog: "God made puppies cute for a reason." You wouldn't tolerate their behavior otherwise. Even evolutionary theory suggests that humans are biologically predisposed to want to nurture puppies. The roundness of their eyes and heads will elicit a parental-type response from most people. This cuteness is, in fact, what brought early man (and woman) to domesticate dogs in the first place. So don't fall prey to the cute trap; I promise—it wears off!

My friend, Jane, a cool single mom, has an amazingly well-behaved seven-year-old Labrador named Petey and an adorable young "Min Pin" named Sanchez. Sanchez was recently having a few problems, so I recommended crating and tethering him in the house. I figured this was all going to be new to Jane, but instead, it was like a light went on in her head. "Oh yeah," she told me, "Petey ate an entire couch when he was a puppy and the trainer instructed me to do these same things." Petey, who now sleeps twenty out of twenty-four hours, was so rambunctious that he literally ate a couch!

For a young single person who doesn't have the means to refurbish their apartment or spend every waking minute caring for and monitoring a pup (puppies, like babies, don't always sleep through the night; they miss their littermates and their mother), I strongly suggest you consider an older dog. "No, I want a puppy!" you're probably thinking, but stop and reconsider: Why do you want a puppy so badly? I know they're cute, but if you don't think that what they look like when they're older is also cute, then you're going to have some problems. All dogs grow up.

Besides, older dogs are awesome! I promise. Here's a great list adapted from the Senior Dog Project (*www.srdogs.com*) that says it all. Older dogs:

1. Are housebroken
2. Are instant companions
3. Know what "no" means
4. Let you sleep through the night
5. Let you have a life (something all-important for someone in the dating scene!)

Now, when I say older, there is a range of dogs of all ages from which you can choose. There are tons of dogs available from about one year old on up, but, in my opinion, the best dog for a single person is a three- to seven-year-old dog coming through a rescue organization or a good breeder who is familiar with the dog's behavior and personality.

CANINE CONSIDERATION ❖ ❖ ❖

A good dog is a mellow dog; a mellow dog is an older dog. Therefore, an older dog is a good dog. When looking for a dog, especially as a first-time owner, always consider getting an older dog.

Shedding and Allergies

When helping my single friends figure out what kind of dog to get, I often hear, "Maybe I should buy that dog because I really want one that doesn't shed and this one's hypoallergenic." Before you max out your credit card buying a dog from a website or store claiming they have nonshedding, hypoallergenic dogs . . . STOP! There is no such thing as a hypoallergenic, nonshedding dog! All dogs (except hairless ones) shed, and people aren't allergic to pet hair, but to pet dander. All dogs, whether furry, curly haired, or hairless, produce dander.

Let me explain. Yes, there are breeds that shed less than others. Poodles and terriers lose less hair, causing fewer allergies. There are two main reasons for this: First, they have less hair to lose because they either don't have an undercoat or they have a minimal one; second, the hair they do have stays put. In the case of Silkies and Yorkies, their hair just continues to grow longer and longer, and for curly haired dogs like Poodles and Welsh Terriers, their loose hair gets trapped in the curl of their coat. Either situation keeps these breeds' loose hair, and the accompanying dander, with the dogs.

An owner can also achieve a lower-shed, lower-allergy-provoking dog if she is willing to put a little effort into it. Even super-sheddy dogs like Labradors or Golden Retrievers can be less messy if given regular baths and frequent brushing to remove dander and loose hair. A particularly fabulous tool in the shedding battle is the Furminator (*www.furminator.com*). Developed by a professional groomer, regular use can reduce shedding up to 90 percent by removing a dog's undercoat and loose hair that would otherwise end up on your floor, causing allergies. When I have been diligent with the Furminator (which I'm not always, by the way), Bella has been almost shed free.

To augment the allergy-fighting power of frequent brushing and regular baths, wipe your dog down after walks or visits to the dog park with an antidander wipe such as Quick Bath Cleansing Wipes. These handy items help cut down on dander buildup as well as dog saliva, which is another allergy-causing culprit.

CANINE CONSIDERATION ❖ ❖ ❖

There is no such thing as a hypoallergenic dog. All dogs can cause allergies because all dogs produce dander. Terriers, Poodles, and Bichons, however, do shed less, sending less dander into the air and causing fewer allergies.

Now, I'm not unrealistic here. I am certain many of you have read this chapter and are still set on the same breed you were before you read word one. I get it. It is hard to be open to anything but that little face in your mind's eye. And maybe the breed you have in mind is the perfect dog for you. But maybe it's not. All I ask is that you keep an open mind and do a little research.

three

finding your dream dog

Once you have chosen the perfect breed for your life, whether it's a Mastiff, "Min Pin," or mutt, there are still decisions to be made. Most importantly, how you are going to get that dog? A disclaimer here: I am a dog rescuer and admittedly super biased. I feel that rescue is by far the best option when getting a dog. Now that that's out in the open, I also understand rescue isn't going to work for every single owner-to-be.

The road to choosing a dog is filled with a lot of misinformation, myths, and things most people probably don't even know about shelters, rescue groups, breeders, and pet stores. To help you choose the path that makes sense for you, here are the realities of each alternative, some advice and lessons learned, plus a few great stories of how some owners have ended up with their canine cohorts.

CANINE CONSIDERATION ❖ ❖ ❖

Choose the path to getting your dog that makes most sense to you. Just be sure you've considered all the options.

The Shelter and the Pound

An animal shelter is a facility that houses homeless, lost, or abandoned animals. An animal is kept at a shelter until it is reclaimed by an owner, adopted to a new owner, placed with another organization, or euthanized.

Contrary to popular belief, animal shelters house all kinds of dogs, both purebred and mixed, of all ages. I have personally rescued everything from adorable mutts to an eight-week-old Maltese puppy to countless rare, purebred Mastiffs, all from Los Angeles–area shelters. Just because a dog is a fancy or expensive breed doesn't mean it can't end up in the shelter.

Similarly, it's a myth that dogs in shelters have done something wrong to end up there. Some dogs do end up in shelters due to behavioral or health issues, but a large percentage of shelter dogs are there through no fault of their own. Often, people bring in dogs for incredibly stupid reasons: The Maltese puppy was dropped off on a family's way out of town for a trip; they didn't want to take it with them and they didn't know when they'd be back. A sweet German Shepherd was brought in because he kept trying to kiss his owner while she was sunbathing and it was getting in the way of her achieving an even tan. You get the idea. While pets are becoming more and more central to our lives, we have a disposable culture where people get sick of things and move on. Some people will even bring in one dog and leave with another one. It's vile, but it happens.

According to the Humane Society, one of every four dogs in U.S. animal shelters is a purebred.

The Good News about Shelters

Shelters save lives. Most Animal Control officers care deeply about animals and willingly deal with the pain and sadness of their job so they can see animals adopted into happy homes or saved by rescue groups.

There are all kinds of dogs at the shelter and often shelters will have mixed-breed puppies. Due to the fact that raising a litter of puppies borders on somewhere between hell and having your teeth cleaned, many people bring in nursing moms or pregnant dogs. These are often the absolute best puppies on earth! As my vet says, the path to getting the best dog is to let "God take over and let dogs interbreed. Good old-fashioned mutts are always going to be healthier."

Some shelters provide their dogs with some form of basic medical care, and will provide adopters with antibiotics if the dog has an upper respiratory infection, something very common in shelter dogs. Most shelters also provide low-cost or free-with-adoption vaccinations and microchipping.

The Bad News about Shelters

It's important to know that shelters are different from Humane Societies. Humane Societies are run privately, are usually no-kill or low-kill organizations, and can attempt to accept only animals they think they can place with new owners. Shelters are run by cities or counties and must accept all animals, which is why they will eventually, some sooner than others, euthanize even healthy animals to make room in their facilities.

Due to overcrowding, shelter workers can only do so much to care for dogs and assess their behavior. You might be getting a dog that you know very little about, and will have no recourse other than taking the dog back to the shelter and an uncertain fate if things don't work out. Between the stress of being at a shelter and being exposed to illnesses, shelter dogs may also need additional medical care upon adoption.

DOGMA:

Getting Your Pet

Petfinder.com **is** an online database of homeless pets in the care of about 10,000 animal welfare organizations in the United States, Canada, and beyond. The site has facilitated 10 million adoptions in its first ten years. At any one time, 200,000 pets are listed—dogs, cats, rabbits, birds, and more. Users can search by kind of animal, breed, gender, size, and age. The results are ranked in proximity to the user's zip code. Each shelter and rescue group has its own home page and pet list on the site, and the pets even have their own pages with a description and photo. Shelter personnel and volunteers keep the lists of pets updated, so the available pets change daily.

Initial Cost

Most shelters operate on a first-come, first-served basis, where the first person there can adopt a dog and pay the adoption fee—which can vary from $5 to $100—with very few questions. At some shelters, if multiple people are vying for a dog, the shelter will set up a bidding situation to raise much-needed funds, where each party interested in a particular dog can bid against one another. I witnessed one such auction for a cat that went up to $400, and have heard about auctions exceeding $1,000 for a dog.

What's Covered?

Every shelter is different, but there are usually a few components to an adoption fee. There is the fee itself for the adoption, and then the cost of vaccines, microchipping, and spaying or neutering. Some shelters roll it all into one amount while others have a separate clinic where you pay for the surgery and the vaccines. If you adopt a previously spayed or neutered dog, your cost will be significantly lower.

Follow-Up Cost

The cost to bring home a shelter dog can vary greatly. Some shelter dogs will come home happy and healthy while others will need more extensive medical care for common post-shelter ailments such as upper respiratory illness, stomach bug, or skin issues. The cost for these will depend on the severity and where you live, but is often less than buying a dog, and the reward for investing this money is a dog that will be forever grateful and indebted to you.

Resources

All cities and counties contract with a shelter to deal with animal issues ranging from stray pets to wild critters. To find your local shelter, go to your city or county website for a link. Most shelters will have photos of their available dogs online. If you see a dog you like, either call or go to the shelter and ask to speak with an adoption coordinator to discuss adoption.

Another way to find shelter dogs is to check out online databases such as *www.petfinder.org*, *www.adoptapet.com*, and *www.petharbor.com*. Adoption coordinators post dogs on these sites as a way to reach out to people who might not otherwise come to their specific shelter. The databases allow users to search by zip code, breed, and age.

While some shelters rely on the Internet alone, their most common outreach tool is the adoption fair. Mobile adoption events provide shelters with a great way to network their adoptable dogs and adoption fees are often lower for you. You can check on shelter websites to find adoption-fair dates and locations.

─────────────── **Nancy and Rhett** ───────────────

Nancy and I had worked together for about a year—a year of me dragging her to adoption events and drafting her into helping me with beg letters for donations—when it was finally time for her to get a dog. She moved from a condo into a house and her first priority was to put up a fence to make her house dog-ready. With friends like me, and because her family adopted a wonderful dog from the pound when she was a child, Nancy knew she wanted to rescue. Like so many owners-to-be, she found herself visiting all of the local groups' websites, perusing the profiles of all the great dogs for adoption. A month later, the fence was up and she couldn't wait—she filled out an online application. It was approved, and that Saturday afternoon she went to visit an adorable Australian Shepherd named Houston. All she needed was to wait for the home check to be done.

One Sunday morning, there happened to be a mobile adoption event for L.A. Animal Services ("the pound") at her local PETCO. "I stopped by 'just to see.' And there he was: the most handsome boy ever, with long wavy hair, a gorgeous tail, and floppy ears. He picked me! I don't know how else to say it. I saw him, took him for a short walk, and fell in love."

Well, kind of. Nancy was actually quite torn. She felt this dog was remarkable, but also felt a commitment to Houston, the dog at the rescue she had visited the day before. Nancy told the animal services people that she'd be back—something many people say but never do, by the way—and headed off to think. A bit overwhelmed, Nancy called me and we talked through it. Yes, she had "put her name" on Houston, but we knew that he was "safe" at a good rescue where he would never be put down and would likely be placed into a deserving and loving home. This other big lug of a dog—a large German Shepherd or Leonberger mix with intense eyes—was not so safe. It was quite likely that if Nancy didn't take him, he'd be back at the shelter facing an uncertain future. Once Nancy realized Houston would be safe, she beelined it back to the adoption fair and took her big guy home.

Rescue Groups

A rescue organization or group is an affiliation of volunteers who save dogs and find homes for them. Groups run the gamut from large-scale operations like Best Friends Sanctuary in Utah to individuals who rescue one dog at a time. Rescue is not a glamorous business; most groups don't have their own facility and will either keep a dog in a "foster home" or pay to board a dog at a kennel, vet hospital, or doggie day care until that dog is adopted. No matter what, these dogs should be well taken care of. Rescue groups often obtain animals from local animal shelters as well as from owners who can no longer keep a dog. Some groups are breed-specific and tied to national breed clubs while other groups rescue mixed breeds and purebreds of different varieties.

What Kind of Dogs Can I Find Through Rescue?

Most breeds are available for adoption through rescue groups—even breeds you think are too cute, too rare, or too expensive to be given up. Mutts are always available for adoption. Dogs of all ages are also available. While there are tons of mixed-breed puppies available through rescues, there are fewer purebred puppies than might be available through a breeder. However, there are many young dogs (one to two years old) available in rescue because so many people get puppies and then give them up when they're no longer little.

The Good News about Rescue Groups

Rescue groups will know more about the dogs they place than the average shelter because the dogs have been fostered in homes or cared for in boarding facilities, getting more one-on-one attention. Rescuers should be able to tell you how the dog will interact with other pets, children, and strangers and, if things don't work out for you and a dog, you can bring a dog back to a rescue and know that she will be safe. Additionally, dogs from rescue groups will be vaccinated, spayed or neutered, and microchipped.

The Bad News about Rescue Groups

Rescuers can come off as a bit intense and appear as if they are grilling you, which they probably are. It's important to know that it's not personal; they do this in hopes of making sure their dogs don't end up back in bad situations. They have you fill out applications, give references, and agree to home checks as a way to screen out undesirable homes. Many times, rescuers will ask an applicant if they rent or own. Although a seemingly personal question, especially for a single person who may not own their own place, know that rescuers have their reasons. They are often hesitant to adopt to people who rent because one of the most common reasons people give up dogs is that they have to move and can only find a no-pets-accepted apartment.

Another common rescue-related problem is that some rescuers won't disclose a dog's issues, either because a dog hasn't shown this behavior while in rescue or because the rescuer doesn't want to jeopardize a dog's chance of finding a home. The best way to combat this issue is not to be afraid to ask them as many questions as they're asking you! Remember, the more info you know the better.

No matter whom you rescue from, there is the possibility that a rescue dog has come from a neglectful or abusive situation. Rescue groups can only do so much to rehab behaviorally and physically, although most rescues have a policy never to adopt out a sick dog. A good rescue group will help you navigate this situation and some will split medical costs, but if you're going to rescue be prepared to spend some time helping your dog overcome the upheavals of their past.

Resources

Most rescue groups have a website where they feature the dogs they currently have in rescue. You can find these sites by searching on Google for your breed of choice along with the area in which you live, contacting that breed's local breed club or going to *www.petfinder.com* or *www.1-800-save-a-pet.com*. Social networking sites like *www.dogster.com*, *www.facebook.com*, and *www.myspace.com* can also provide amazing ways to connect with dogs who you would never otherwise meet.

▼ Tips on Finding Your Perfect Dog Online

Just as with online dating, it's best to read a rescue dog's online profile extremely carefully. Here are a few things to keep in mind:

1. **Take Everything with a Grain of Salt.** We've all heard the proverbial story of a girl showing up to a blind date with a guy whose profile says he works out five days a week, but who actually has a belly like Santa Claus, or the girl who has miraculously gained twenty pounds since her picture was taken. In much the same way, rescuers try to put a positive spin on a dog they want someone to adopt. While I'm not implying that rescuers lie, I will say that they love the dogs they rescue and want them to get into good homes.

2. **Don't Just Look at the Picture.** Pictures are worth a thousand words, but you *must* read a dog's profile and look at their likes and dislikes. Do they like kids? Other dogs? Cats? Of course it's important to like the way a dog looks, but the profile will tell you how a dog will behave.

3. **Key Words.** Just as there are certain phrases in dating profiles which should be red flags—"Life of the party" means she won't shut up . . . ever and "forty-two and just haven't found the right one yet" means he's a commitment-phobe—there are certain key words or phrases in dog profiles that indicate there may be more going on than a rescuer wants to come right out and say.

For instance:

- "Spirited," "high energy," and "needs stimulation" all pretty much mean hyper.
- "In need of compassion and understanding" may mean that dog has some shyness or behavioral issues.
- "You have to go a little slow with him at first, but once he knows you he's just a bouncy, fun, playful dog" may mean that he bites strangers.
- "Must have a secure fence" could mean that the dog is an escape artist.

Key words don't always indicate bigger issues, but it is your job to ask questions about a dog before you decide to bring him or her home. A rescuer is more apt to give you the straight goods on a dog once you have them in a one-on-one e-mail exchange, on the phone, or face to face. Similarly, they may have a better dog in mind for you based on your lifestyle, so be open to suggestions.

Alyson and Lucia

My friend Alyson is the essence of east-side, Los Angeles. Think art galleries, loft parties, and urban pioneering. When she decided to get a dog, Alyson applied to a rescue group I worked with to adopt a large and rambunctious Neapolitan Mastiff named Nemo. Knowing Nemo wasn't a good fit for her (she needed a mellow dog), I suggested one of our other dogs; an older girl named Lucia. She was four years old—a perfect age for a Neapolitan—and was mellow and friendly with strangers.

Thankfully, Alyson was open to my suggestion and I'm happy to report that four years later, Lucia and Alyson are still going strong.

Breeder

A breeder is either a person or a facility that breeds dogs. Under AKC (American Kennel Club) rules, the breeder is the owner or the lessee of the dam (the mother) on the date of a mating that results in a litter.

What Kind of Dog Can I Find at a Breeder?

Puppies of all breeds are available from breeders and some breeders will also have adult dogs available that have been kept for breeding or showing.

The Good News about Breeders

The good news is that reputable breeders do exist. There are some outstanding and caring (usually small-scale) breeders who, out of a deep love for a particular breed, raise healthy puppies they care deeply about in both the short and long term.

The Bad News about Breeders

Breeding can be quite a shady business. Many breeders—not all, but many—are chiefly concerned with profit, and have little regard for the health and welfare of the dogs involved. Breeding is often done by so-called "backyard breeders" (the commonly accepted term for random or ignorant breeding conducted on a small scale) and "puppy mills" or "puppy farms" (larger businesses), where animals are kept under the most inhumane conditions. These disreputable breeders will often mate dogs regardless of heredity issues such as hip dysplasia, predisposition for cancer, or skin issues. Some breeders will also sell you dogs they know may be sick or sickly, and there is little recourse. Breeders have been known to tell a new owner of such a puppy to simply euthanize it and they will send them a new one!

Things to Look Out For

Online sales and classified ads selling puppies are often bad news. This is a red flag that these dogs aren't coming from the happy place displayed on a website or in an ad. Reputable breeders will not sell their dogs this way; they may have a website, but you can't place an order sight unseen.

When purchasing a puppy, go to the breeder, meet the puppy's parents, and see what kind of condition the dog has been raised in. Ask to see where the puppies live. Is the environment clean? Are the adult dogs well cared for? Remember, just because a dog has papers doesn't mean it comes from a good breeder. To find a reputable breeder, get references from your vet, the local rescue

DOGMA:

Beware of Breeders

Unscrupulous and uninformed breeders seek to keep up with demand and breed without regard to issues of temperament or health. This undermines the mental and physical health of a significant percentage of (but not all) purebred dogs.

finding your dream dog

club for your chosen breed, or go to regional dog shows to see who's winning. Ask if they have litters coming up or if they can recommend other breeders who do.

Initial Cost
$400–$5,000 depending on pedigree and demand for a breed.

Resources
The American Kennel Club (*www.akc.org*) is an organization that promotes "the sport of purebred dogs and breeding for type and function." The AKC recognizes over 150 different dog breeds and sanctions more than 18,500 dog shows and events each year, including the nationally televised Eukanuba National Championships. According to the AKC website, "The AKC is the only purebred dog registry in the U.S. that conducts kennel inspections to ensure the health, safety and welfare of dogs." However, it is important to know that having a dog with AKC papers does not guarantee that he is a healthy or well-bred puppy. The AKC makes a concerted effort to keep the integrity of the kennels they sanction high, but the demand is too great. Breeders can register their litters without any AKC inspection; often, neither the puppies nor the environment in which they are raised will be examined or approved.

For these reasons, it's best to be like our friend Shelly. Remember her?

Shelly and Sadie

Shelly created a mutt map and decided that she wanted a very young purebred Cavalier King Charles Spaniel puppy. So, with the same intensity Shelly put toward selecting her perfect breed, she researched Cavalier King Charles breeders.

*Aware of the many unscrupulous breeders, Shelly signed up for a Cavalier bulletin board, read articles, surveyed breed-club websites and, most helpfully, went to dog shows in her area. She met various Cavalier breeders and fanciers and asked around until she found Donna and her kennel—Beauty & Beast Kennels (***www.beautynbeast.net***). Donna has been wonderful and has even given me a bit of faith in breeders.*

Donna is an example of a model breeder. She only breeds one to two litters a year, has a great track record of avoiding genetic health issues (Cavalier King Charles Spaniels frequently have heart conditions), and most of all she has an open-door policy, welcoming all potential buyers to visit her home and breeding facility. Moreover, Donna's purchase contract stipulates that if, at any point in a dog's life, the owner is unable to care for the dog, the

DOGMA:

Personal Placement

"A reputable breeder never sells puppies to a pet shop or broker, but only through direct contact with the final owner, in order to properly match the dog to the owner and ensure that the owner is ready for the responsibility of dog ownership and can provide a safe and proper home." —*www.Papillonclub.org*

finding your dream dog

dog must be returned to her. This woman really embodies what you want to look for in a breeder; she truly cares for her puppies, far beyond any sense of profit—something I respect, admire, and wish more breeders emulated.

Pet Store

Thanks to Oprah's amazing informational exposés on puppy mills, the deplorable conditions the animals live in, and the corrupt trade these breeders engage in, most people now know to avoid purchasing dogs from just anyone. However, no one sets out to buy a puppy-mill dog. The sad fact is that most pet stores, no matter what they may tell you, have gotten their puppies from a questionable source.

The great news is that popular pet supply stores like PETCO and PetSmart don't sell dogs! In fact, each chain spends millions of dollars a year to help stem the tide of unwanted dogs through robust rescue education and spay/neuter programs. Many of these popular stores even host adoption events sponsored by shelters, rescues, and the Humane Society so you'll know more about the dog that you're welcoming into your home.

What Kind of Dog Can I Get at a Pet Store?

Pet stores usually sell only young puppies—either purebreds or what's known as designer dogs. Designer dogs are crosses of popular breeds and have names like "Lhasa-poos," "Puggles," or just about any other combination you can think of. These dogs often come from backyard breeders or puppy mills because a reputable breeder would not allow their dogs to be sold this way.

The Good News about Pet Stores

There isn't much good news. Even breed clubs recommend that people not buy dogs from pet stores. There are a handful of pet stores that do take an interest in where their pets go, but for the most part their dogs are strictly a commodity.

The Bad News about Pet Stores

Responsible breeders simply do not sell dogs to pet stores, so the majority of dogs you find there will likely be from disreputable breeders or puppy mills where dogs are often abused and treated inhumanely. For more information, go to *www.stoppuppymills.org*. Many of these pet stores may unknowingly get dogs from such places because they deal with brokers or middlemen who facilitate pet sales.

Initial Cost

The cost of a pet-store pup will vary from as little as $300 if a dog has gotten too old (sometimes that may only be six months old) to upwards of $3,000 or even more. Remember, price is no indication of the value or health of a dog. Pet-store dogs are often extremely sick, as Laura experienced. Here is her story.

─────────── **Laura and Lou-Lou** ───────────

Laura had been dying to get a Maltese for years. One day, she stopped by a pet shop she'd passed many times on her way back and forth from work and there she was—a tiny white puff of Maltese sweetness. Laura named her new puppy Lou-Lou and headed home.

Lou-Lou seemed perfectly healthy and responsive that first day, but just to be safe, Laura scheduled a vet visit for Lou-Lou the following

finding your dream dog

day. Sadly, upon reading Lou-Lou's vital signs, the vet informed Laura that Lou-Lou most likely had an aggressive viral condition and very little chance of survival. Devastated and of course already attached, Laura was determined to do everything in her power to save Lou-Lou. She wound up staying at home with a humidifier and syringes, having to force-feed Lou-Lou every two hours for six full days (and nights) before Lou-Lou was even able to stand up. It then took one month before Lou-Lou could eat on her own.

Thankfully, Lou-Lou made it through just fine. But Laura blames the pet shop 100 percent for not providing Lou-Lou with the proper shots or a hygienic environment.

Follow-Up Cost

Laura and Lou-Lou's is not a unique story. Of course, dogs coming from shelters and rescue groups can also have health problems, but you are saving these dogs to begin with—not forking over hundreds or thousands of dollars to be unexpectedly saddled with the emotional and financial responsibility of a sick dog.

How you get your dog is important. Be sure to educate yourself about where you are getting your dog before you make the commitment to bring them home.

So, now that you know how to pick your breed and are familiar with where you can get a dog, it's time to take the leap and bring home the dog of your dreams.

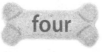

four

starting out on the right paw: training basics

As an owner-to-be preparing to get a dog, it's quite common to find yourself lost in thought about what bringing home your new canine companion will be like. Sure, you know there may be some accidents and the possibility of a chewed shoe or two, but you are an adult; you've done your research, made a decision, and are ready for the commitment. Besides, your dog will be a good dog. Right?

I get excited when my friends find themselves in this state. Unfortunately, I also end up sounding like the fun police, killing their buzz by letting them in on a little secret.

The First Days

Bringing home a dog is exciting, but the early days with any new dog, be it a puppy or adult, can be rough. In the dog business there is a saying: If a dog doesn't pee, poo, vomit, or destroy something in your house within the first forty-eight hours, something is probably wrong with it. This is an exaggeration, but only slightly.

Just as being responsible for another creature's well-being will most likely be a leap for you, coming into a new home will be an equally huge transition for a dog, any dog—puppies to senior citizens, championship blood lines to those whose lineage is a little more dubious. Dogs can't discuss their feelings about the transition from wherever they came (even if it was awful), and instead may display their feelings in peculiar and sometimes off-putting ways. Before you freak out and think you have an insurmountable issue on your hands, relax and keep reading.

Sleeping

When dogs, especially shelter dogs or those who have come from high-stress environments, transition into the peaceful haven of your home, they will often pass out and sleep as though they haven't in weeks. While lethargy is never a good sign, having a dog that sleeps a lot is not something to worry about. They should perk up within a few days, and then their true personalities will emerge—for better or worse.

Separation Anxiety

When a dog comes into a new home, it is normal for him to want to be with you at all times. Dogs often follow their new owner from room to room and will launch into full panic mode if you leave, barking, crying, going to the bathroom in inappropriate places, and tearing things up until you return. Thankfully, this behavior should decrease as the dog gets a better sense of his surroundings and trusts that you're coming back.

To help him build up trust, it is best to crate train him from day one and help desensitize him to the trauma of your absence. I discuss crate training in more detail later on, but trust me, it will be the ultimate key to living out your dream of having that perfectly behaved dog. This is something my friend Marc learned the hard way.

Marc and Sierra

When Marc first got his Golden Retriever Sierra, he never left her alone for more than one minute in the first two weeks. Not surprisingly, the first time he did leave her alone in his apartment, going to Thanksgiving dinner at a friend's house, Sierra went ballistic in a fit of separation anxiety. Marc really hadn't thought ahead. He hadn't crate trained her or confined her in any way, nor had he practiced leaving her and coming back. He simply walked out the door and hoped for the best. He didn't even leave a treat to keep her busy. Growing up, his family's dogs had just taken care of themselves and he figured that since he'd had Sierra for two weeks at that point, how bad could it be?

Well, pretty bad. She scratched up the door and the walls, broke the front door handle, and cried nonstop for hours. Marc's neighbor tried to reach him, but he was out of cell range and never got the call. As he drove home and his cell came back into range, it lit up with message upon message from his neighbor. Marc raced home like a crazy person. When he arrived, everything was eerily quiet. According to the neighbor, Sierra had stopped crying about thirty minutes earlier, but as soon as Marc opened the door, she went insane. She alternated between crawling into his lap and running around the apartment in a distraught fit; she was inconsolable for about fifteen minutes. It was awful and, sadly, it was damaging to the little bit of confidence she had built up over the previous two weeks. It took weeks longer for Marc to be able to leave her for even a second without her freaking out. His inability to properly accustom her to being alone had traumatized her and made the process of leaving her again that much more difficult for both of them.

Luckily, you can rebuild trust with a dog. With a little work and crate training, Sierra began to trust Marc and trust that he was always going to come back. Within a short(ish) period of time, he was able to leave her for longer and longer. Now, years later, she barely notices when Marc leaves, and the excitement she displays when he comes home is as much about her getting dinner as it is about him being there. Don't be discouraged if this independence doesn't happen overnight—all dogs go through pretty bad separation anxiety in the first few days.

Odd Potty Behavior

Dogs commonly express anxiety over a change in environment by engaging in some odd potty habits. When my friend, Nell, brought her new dog Humphrey home, he didn't pee or poop for the first twenty-four hours. On the other hand, some previously housebroken dogs will have accidents within the first few days of moving into a new home. They are either marking their territory or are nervous about the change and are acting out accordingly. (My friend Amanda's Chihuahua, Rocky, climbed up on her bed and peed on her favorite pillow.) There is also the possibility that a dog simply isn't potty trained at all.

Whatever the case may be, you can introduce or reinforce good potty behavior by crate training your dog, and never punishing a dog for peeing or pooping inside unless you catch him in the act. Also, be sure to clean up his mess with a product like Nature's Miracle or a similar bacteria-eating solution. Dogs will often re-mark the exact location they have peed on before, so it's best to remove the scent immediately.

Running Away

It is extremely common, especially for rescue dogs, to run away soon after they first come to a new home. Even if their last residence was just this side of hell on earth, it was something they were familiar with and they may try to find their way back. I recently caught a gorgeous German Shepherd puppy running

DOGMA:

The First Few Days

When bringing home a new dog, it's a good idea to give your neighbors a friendly heads-up. Let them know that you've gotten a new dog and that there may be some barking and crying, and that you apologize in advance.

through traffic. Thankfully, she was still wearing tags for the rescue group that had placed her and they had a contact number. The dog's name was Lilly and she had been placed only ninety minutes before, but had slipped out the door as her new owner picked up a piece of mail on the stoop. I'm sure the only reason she finally stopped for me was that she was tired of running.

To prevent this situation from happening to you, keep a new dog safely confined to a crate or smaller room such as the bathroom whenever she's left alone. Also, be sure to keep your new pooch away from open doors and gates at all times.

Chewing and Destruction

Part of getting a dog is dealing with the inevitable destruction they bring. I'm not suggesting you condone destructive dog behavior, but when getting a dog—especially a puppy—there is not only a distinct possibility, but rather a probability that your dog will destroy something you care about or that has value. Do you remember Petey the Labrador, who ate an entire couch? Another friend's puppy ate through her front door, and when my friend Michael took his dog Murphy to Wyoming, Murphy ate the corner of his friend's ridiculously expensive Oriental rug.

Puppies and even older dogs often turn to chewing to soothe anxiety. Chewing behavior, therefore, tends to be worst in the first few days of bringing a dog home, when anxiety is highest. Given a choice to chew or not chew or to root or not root through your underwear drawer, a young dog or an anxious dog will most likely choose badly. So particularly in the first few weeks with a dog, be sure to create environments in which your dog can succeed. Don't leave things out for your dog to destroy. Just as you wouldn't hand the keys to your car over to a seven-year-old, you shouldn't leave a dog unsupervised with free access to items they can destroy.

Taking the Lead

Don't forget your part in all this. You'd be somewhat of an anomaly in canine ownership if bringing home a dog didn't stress you out. That said, I encourage you to let things go as much as possible and simply try to enjoy the company of your new dog. Dogs pick up on human anxiety and it compounds their own. So, be playful, affectionate, and loving—the weird behavior of the first few days will most likely pass.

Building a Successful Relationship with Your Dog

Just as being mellow in the first few days while a dog transitions to a new environment is essential, so too is establishing yourself as a confident dog owner for the long run. You're probably wondering how in the world you're supposed to be confident when you have no idea what you're doing. The answer is simple—dog training.

Basic Training

Dog training is a somewhat vague and all-encompassing term. It can mean everything from "sit, stay, come, shake" to a more general definition of teaching a dog how to be a good team player—not peeing on your floor, nipping people, and or having destructive separation anxiety. Defining your idea of what having a trained dog means plus determining how much work you are willing to put toward your training effort will narrow your choices and help you pick a training regimen. Establish some concrete training goals. If teaching your dog to shake isn't on your priority list, don't waste your time.

New owners often ask my opinion on trainers, training facilities, dog and puppy classes, and popular training books. However, there isn't one single method of dog training guaranteed to work for all dogs or all owners. Instead, the day-to-day realities of the plan must work for you and your dog in order for it to work overall.

Owners often look at me and say, "Okay, that's nice, but how do you know which method to choose and, more specifically, which trainer to trust?" You make that choice by weighing all your options and considering the two main variables of dog training, what I call method and delivery. *Method* relates to the ideology of the training and *delivery* to how training is implemented.

▼ **Choose a Method, Choose a Trainer**

Method relates to how the trainer or training path achieves its goal of turning out a trained dog. Does the practice rely on positive reinforcement, in which dogs are rewarded and given treats for good behavior, or is the dog reprimanded with physical and or verbal cues? Training often uses a combination of positive and negative cues, and it's up to you to decide whether or not the approach feels right. To figure this out, you need to do some homework. Ask your vet and friends to refer you to a trainer and ask any trainer to whom you are referred about their experience and training method. Give them a scenario: If my dog was doing XYZ, how would you instruct me to correct this behavior, and why would that be the right approach? If you are uncomfortable with a trainer or their response or if they are dismissive of your inquiries, move on and find another option.

CANINE CONSIDERATION ❖ ❖ ❖

If you call a trainer and you don't like their demeanor or they won't take five minutes to tell you about their approach, say "buh-bye."

Once you have decided which training methodology you prefer, you must figure out how you want to implement that approach. There are four main ways to train your dog.

1. You can send them off to a training facility.
2. You and your dog can go through one-on-one training.
3. You can take your dog to a dog and puppy class.
4. You can use the numerous books and DVDs out there to create a training regimen of your own.

Remember, no one training approach will work for every dog. Here are the realities, benefits, and drawbacks of the various training options so you can make a choice that works for you and your dog.

Training Camp

Training facilities are programs where you send your dog away and, with any luck, they come home trained. While the particulars vary—some are large-scale facilities and sometimes it is just a trainer who takes in a few dogs at a time—the commonality is that your dog can get a lot of training in a short period of time. However, even though you're not training your dog yourself, the work he did at camp will be for naught if you don't consistently reinforce the lessons your dog has learned when he returns home. So, if you're going to make the investment to train your dog, it's best for everyone if you also make the commitment to follow through.

Cost: $500–$3,000
Time: One week to one month with daily follow-ups

starting out on the right paw: training basics

Best for: Busy people who are able to keep up with the training upon their dog's return; dogs who show any dominance or aggression

Advantages: Provides a good training base for your dog; no matter how bad you are at follow-up, your dog will at least have some training under her collar

Disadvantages: Cost, and you still have to follow up on your own

Private Training

Private training usually involves a trainer coming to your house for either one session or a series of sessions to train both you and your dog on everything from basic obedience to problem solving. I am big fan of private training and think it provides the most bang for your buck and a very personalized experience for you and your dog. When it's just you, your dog, and a trainer, you can work on your dog's specific challenges. Moreover, private lessons at home are preferable because home is where the pee and the destruction happen. A trainer can witness the offensive behaviors, show you how to stop them, and reinforce good behavior.

Cost: $50–$150 per hour (some trainers have a flat rate for a three-hour session or a series of five sessions)

Time: Expect to spend two to five hours with a trainer, then daily follow-ups

Best for: All new owners, but especially those whose dogs are experiencing specific challenges such as housebreaking, separation anxiety, or destructive behavior

Advantages: Personalized attention for your dog's specific needs

Disadvantages: Can get pricey

Dog and Puppy Classes

Independent trainers, animal control agencies, and pet stores across the country—including PETCO and PetSmart—offer dog and puppy classes. Class format varies and some classes are geared specifically for puppies, others for older dogs, but the end goal for all classes will be the same: creating a better line of communication between dog and owner. While private instruction may be advantageous because you can focus on your dog's unique issues, group classes offer the distinct advantage of working with your dog on important behavioral issues while in a social environment. Classes provide a safe environment for you to reinforce good behaviors while also learning the critical dynamics of dog-to-dog and dog-to-stranger socialization.

Cost: $100–$300 per course

Time: Two hours per week for six to eight weeks with daily follow-ups

Best for: Dogs without major behavioral issues, puppies who need to work on socialization, and owners with the

DOGMA:

Training Tactic

Often, the best plan of attack is to find a good trainer who offers both group classes and private sessions. See if you can get a discount! This way you get the best of both worlds.

discipline to actually commit to a class once a week for six to eight weeks

Advantages: Socialization comes with training

Disadvantages: Not personalized and classes don't always draw the top trainers

DIY Dog Training

Disciplined owners (a category I don't fall into, by the way) can achieve great obedience results by following the books, DVDs, and training manuals of mega dog trainers like Cesar Millan or lesser-known but highly effective trainers such as Tamar Geller (*www.tamargeller.com*) to create a program of their own. By following the lead of an experienced trainer and adapting it to your own lifestyle and your own dog, you will most likely achieve better results than an owner who sends her dog away to an expensive training camp. Why? Because you are doing the heavy lifting from day one. The biggest hurdle is that there are no appointments to make or classes to attend. The discipline—and consistency—must come from within you or you'll be in big trouble.

Cost: Free (if checked out from your local library) to $100 for multimedia training package

Time: Daily implementation for six to eight weeks

Best for: Disciplined owners

Advantages: Cost and flexibility

Disadvantages: You are not an expert; dog may be giving you cues or engaging in behavior that you may not realize is a problem

Make One or Make Them All Work for You

The best thing an owner can do is create a combination of the aforementioned options, which are endless. There is, however, one option that's off the table, and that's choosing not to train your dog at all!

Dogs may live in our human world, but they interpret and deal with that world differently. Training helps bridge the gap between our world and theirs. Most unwanted canine behavior comes from fear or anxiety about who is leading the pack. If you are not the leader of your pack (the alpha), your dog will feel uneasy. For some dogs, this can lead to aggressive behavior, for others destruction and chewing. Training supports the owner-as-alpha message, and asking a dog to work for everything it wants makes sense to them and makes them feel safe. While this may seem a little militaristic, it is actually the best way to build up your dog's confidence in himself and, more importantly, in you.

Potty Training

Lack of potty training is one of the most common reasons dogs and puppies are given up.

Unfortunately, while having a potty-trained dog is certainly preferable, getting your dog through the process can be daunting. It can take dogs weeks to get the hang of potty training, and for puppies—especially the smaller breeds—holding their business for more than a couple of hours is biologically challenging until they're full grown. And to make things just a little more maddening, dogs will often take one step forward only to start having accidents again a few weeks later; like I said, frustrating.

Biological challenges aside, realize that potty training will be a new concept for previously untrained dogs and puppies. Simply providing a dog with access to a potty-appropriate location such as a wee-wee pad or outside on a grass spot will help, but won't be enough to convince most dogs that doing their business in those locations is preferable to doing them in your closet.

To instill this very important behavior in your pup, here are some ground rules:

1. Give any untrained dog or puppy ample opportunity to succeed by taking her outside on a frequent basis. Or, if you are using an indoor system such as a wee-wee pad or an indoor grass patch, give her access to that spot, even by placing her right on the pad or the grass regularly throughout the day. This provides her an opportunity to go potty in the right place all the time, rather than setting her up for failure by limiting her access.

2. When your dog relieves himself where he's supposed to, praise him, then praise him some more. Dogs will always want to repeat whatever behavior gets a positive response from the most important person in their lives—you.

3. Interrupt, but never punish. If you catch your dog relieving herself in an inappropriate location, it is best to interrupt the behavior with a firm but calm, "No." Then bring her to an appropriate location to continue her business and say, "Good dog." Never, under any circumstances, drag your dog to a previous potty accident, push her nose in it, and yell at her. She will understand that you're mad, but won't make the connection. Instead, you'll be making her anxious and fearful, without giving her solid direction.

4. Crates are a potty-training owner's best friend. You may not be able to explain to your dog why it's a bad idea for him to use your bed as a pee post, but you can tap into canine psychology to achieve your potty-training goals. Dogs like to keep their immediate area clean, so keeping a dog in a confined area like a crate will take advantage of this ingrained canine behavior and help him control his potty urges. Using a crate facilitates potty training far more than just following ground rules one through three.

CANINE CONSIDERATION ❖ ❖ ❖

Potty training can be challenging. Be patient and clear to give your dog every opportunity to succeed by using a crate, giving her ample access to appropriate potty locales, and never reprimanding her unless you catch her in the act.

Crate Training

The basic idea behind crate training is this: Your pooch may not look or act much like one, but even the tiniest of dogs are, at their core, wolves in dog collars. As such, their canine instinct as den-dwelling animals should make them feel most comfortable and safe when in a secure space such as a crate. Dogs don't live in an egalitarian society; for them, someone always has to be alpha. If not, they will vie for the role or have great anxiety. By restricting them to their crate while you are free, you are cementing their position beneath you, easing anxieties that may otherwise manifest in fun ways such as shredding your couch or obliterating your shoes.

Remember, the key to being a successful owner is figuring out how to care for your dog while maintaining a full, rich life of your own. Being single, we are unfettered by commitments to a partner or to kids; we can move apartments or even cities if we want. We can go out on dates or even sleepovers—if we're lucky! Having a crate-trained dog makes taking advantage of these perks of singlehood more realistic.

Crate training means you can more confidently leave your dog at home (for no longer than six hours for adults; for puppies, one hour for each month of age up to six months) and more easily incorporate them into your single life. Because you can bring your dog's safe place—his crate—to almost any new environment, including your new "friend's" apartment across town, you will be able to do all the fun things your married friends have to ask permission to do, while being confident your dog is safe and happy and is not going to eat your new friend's rug!

So, now that you know crate training is your golden ticket to bliss, be prepared—the process can be dreadful. Realize that you cannot just get a dog, throw him in a crate, leave for hours, and end up with a pup who's potty trained and self-sufficient. If you improperly introduce a dog to crate training, leave him in the crate too long, or use the crate as punishment, you won't get any of the benefits described. Crate training will require a lot of work on your part, and the cry of a dog when he is adjusting to his crate can be awful. But don't be discouraged; you are doing the right thing, for your dog and for yourself.

So, take a leap of faith, know it might get worse before it gets better, and warn your neighbors that the noise won't last long. Here is an overview of what to expect and a few tricks of the trade to get you through crate training with a little less stress.

The best way to create a confident, happy dog is to crate train from day one!

▼ Crate Basics

First, you have to buy a crate. There are several variables when it comes to crates. Let's start with the issue of size.

Size

When choosing a crate, size matters. The basic rule of thumb is to get a crate your dog can stand up and turn around in comfortably. Crates are usually sized by weight and breed, but these are only rough estimates, and you could create an anxiety-producing environment if the crate is too small. Solve this problem by bringing your dog with you. Conversely, don't think that bigger is always better. Crates are huge space eaters, and getting a crate that is too big for your dog can also undermine the

DOGMA:

Crate Smarts

Craigslist.org and garage sales are fantastic ways to find all styles of crates at a discount. Be sure to evaluate the crate before you purchase it. Make sure the latches work properly and all the parts are present, and be sure to pay extra attention to cleanliness.

benefits of crate training. Crates should mimic a den environment for your dog, creating a cozy, safe place. If that space is too big, she won't get that safe feeling, nor will it create a controlled environment in which she won't go potty.

Crates come in a variety of materials including cloth, metal, plastic, and even wicker or hardwoods to better blend with your décor. Each type of crate has benefits as well as drawbacks. They all perform the same basic function of creating a safe haven for your dog, but crates—with prices running $50–$300+—aren't cheap, so do some research to see which kind will work best for you and your pooch.

CANINE CONSIDERATION ❖ ❖ ❖

Bring your dog with you to get the right size crate, one in which your dog can stand up and turn around in comfortably.

▼ The Training Part of Crate Training

Now that you know how to choose the right crate for your dog and the options for buying one, let's talk about how to train. Crate training is best done over a few days. I recommend that people get—and begin training—their dog on a Friday night or the beginning of a long weekend so they don't feel rushed through the process. This way you assert yourself as the pack leader right from the start.

A Simple Step-by-Step Process

1. Set up your crate right in the middle of things, whether that means your living room, your kitchen, or your bedroom—doesn't matter. Just make sure the crate is right where you

are. Dogs are social creatures; beginning the training process with you around will make things easier.

2. Make your dog's crate cozy and inviting. Place a favorite blanket or shirt that you have recently worn that smells like you (and which you are not afraid to sacrifice) inside the crate to make it less foreign to your pooch.

3. Take small but yummy treats and place a few just inside the open door to the crate. Wait for your dog to get the treat, praise him, and allow him to enjoy his reward. Do not try to close him in at this point.

4. Repeat. Place new rations of treats yet a little farther inside the crate. Wait for him to get those treats. Praise him and allow him to reap (eat) his rewards. Then repeat again until he is comfortable going all the way in to the back of the crate.

5. Give your dog a potty break, either here or between other steps. Dogs, especially puppies, must be given an opportunity to relieve themselves outside of the crate. Plus, crate training cannot be forced; food only works as a reward when a dog is hungry. So, go for a walk. Play fetch. Give your dog distractions, a chance to go to the bathroom, and time to get a little hungry. Don't give your dog treats during this break time.

6. Return to the crate with a long-lasting and especially smelly chew treat such as a bully stick or a Kong filled with peanut butter or liver treats. Place this attention grabber at the back of the crate. Let your dog assess the situation without stress and with the crate door open. It's okay if he grabs the treat and then walks outside the crate. Calmly take the treat and place it back inside. You want your dog to associate the crate with everything good: you and treats.

7. When your dog seems sufficiently obsessed with the chew toy, close the crate door, but don't leave the area. Talk on the phone, watch TV, check your e-mail. Just be in the area so your dog doesn't immediately equate going in the crate with you leaving. If he cries, ignore him. It's hard to do, but worth it!

8. Before your dog has finished his treat, take him out of the crate and take the treat away. Take another break. Play outside, change his focus, do what you need to do, but don't give him any treats. Treats only come when your dog is inside his crate. Your dog needs to think, "If crate, then treat," making the inside of the crate a good thing.

9. Return your dog to the crate, give him back his toy, close the door, and try walking out of the room just for ten to twenty seconds, without lingering or fussing over him if he cries. Hopefully, the dog will again be consumed with his treat and

DOGMA:

Praise Your Pooch

Praise is an important aspect of training. Let your dog know he did well with enthusiastic words of praise, reinforced with a glowing smile. He will want to repeat whatever action brought your words of encouragement.

forget you've left. Either way, come back in a nonchalant, calm manner. You don't want him to think you're responding to his cries, thus validating and encouraging that behavior.

10. Repeat step nine, leaving the room and eventually the house for longer and longer periods of time. Let him cry if you need to.

By following these steps—repeatedly if need be—your dog will start to become comfortable with his crate because everything, aside from you leaving, is positive. That said, he may still shriek and cry when you walk out the front door. If you are concerned about his well-being as well as with how much your neighbors hate you, leave a tape recorder behind with a long recording tape to hear how bad the noise really is.

While I am a fan of crate training, it is important to know that not all trainers embrace crating and some dogs simply can't deal with the crate. A dog may be claustrophobic or have had a bad experience in the past. By leaving that tape recorder behind you can get a better sense of your dog's true reaction. It's normal for your dog to cry for a few minutes, but if she cries continuously or starts to panic inside the crate, matters are more serious and you need to change your approach.

The last thing you want to do is force a dog to use a crate if it causes rather than soothes anxiety. You can still get all the benefits of crate training and use the same techniques by replacing the crate with any confined space such as a bathroom, gated-off kitchen, or an Exercise Pen or X-pen—an enclosed fenced-in area that you can set up anywhere in your house.

If these options don't work either, consult your veterinarian. Remember, the idea is to create a safe place for your dog, not send her into an anxiety attack. You also never want to leave your dog crated for long periods of time. Don't mistake crate training for a dog walker or day care. Although it's true that dogs don't experience time like we do, leaving a dog in her crate for too long is inhumane and can be dangerous.

Keeping It Up—a Reality Check

While I may sound like a broken record, the importance of being consistent with a training routine cannot be stressed enough. Dogs thrive on regularity and routine. This is a challenge for all owners, but particularly for singles whose life doesn't otherwise have to be as consistent as someone with kids or a partner. Being single, we get to be beholden unto ourselves and ourselves alone. Getting a dog will change this.

Remember, even the most expensive training simply won't work unless you reinforce it. If you don't want to come home after work and reinforce your dog's training, you may have a harder time incorporating a dog into your life than you thought.

five

vetiquette and your dog's doctor

Having lived through many health challenges with Bella and my parents' dogs, I
have learned a lot about keeping my dog's health
on track. I am extremely vigilant about day-to-
day health, but it is equally important to provide
excellent long-term care for your pooch. Thankfully, I have finally found THE ONE. No, not the
perfect partner; better . . . the perfect vet!

It's essential to have a good relationship with your veterinarian. I am lucky to have had some amazing vets since getting Bella, but have also had a few who left something to be desired.

The Good Vet

My current vet, Dr. Carlsen, is the best! He listens to my concerns and sees that the most important being on earth (my dog) is healthy and happy.

Dr. Carlsen recently saved Bella's life. She woke up one day, couldn't walk straight, didn't want to eat, and her gums were a little white. I freaked and rushed her to his office. By the time we got there, Bella was walking and somewhat normalized. While a lot of vets may have thought I was insane and sent me home, Carlsen calmly examined her and ran a battery of tests. Due to a test that seemed "off," he decided to go in for exploratory surgery. Bella's spleen had in fact burst for no obvious reason, and she was bleeding internally. While I'm not advocating that vets always opt for surgery, Carlsen's knowledge and willingness to listen to me saved Bella's life.

Sadly, there are only a handful of amazing vets, but no one should ever feel stupid asking questions about their dog's health. Nor should you have to feel uncomfortable with the way a vet is handling your dog, which is what happened to my good friend Niko when he brought his dog Byron to the vet.

Niko and Byron

As a new owner, Niko used to get a bit frazzled with every bump and scrape Byron got. At one point, Byron scratched his chin and was bleeding. Panicked at the sight of blood, Niko rushed Byron to the vet and settled for the first available doctor. The day turned out so badly that Niko now refers to this woman as "The Bad Vet" and to that day as "The Incident."

The "bad vet" came into the exam room and reached to examine the scratch on Byron's face with a bit too much verve. Not surprisingly, Byron growled and snapped. He didn't bite her, or anyone else. However, within a nanosecond, the vet had Byron muzzled and proceeded to lecture Niko about how he was a bad owner. She didn't even give Niko a chance to talk, or ask questions about Byron's condition.

Later on, after all the drama, Niko realized that all Byron got was a caution sticker on his chart and a tube of antibiotic cream. Now, small scrapes are cleaned at home, and Niko waits to have Byron seen by his real vet, for whom Byron immediately rolls over and shows his enormous belly.

How to Pick a Good Vet

So, how do you choose a veterinarian before you reach a crisis level and get stuck with someone you don't like? The first step is to get references. Ask your friends, family, a local rescue group, your breeder, or even post a request for referrals on *www.craigslist.org*. Hopefully, one name or even a few names will keep coming up and you can make an appointment. However, even if a vet is referred, trust your instincts and decide what's important to you. Here are some deciding factors:

Experience

Are you more comfortable with a vet who has been doing this for years and has seen it all but might be set in his or her ways or is a younger vet familiar with cutting-edge techniques more your speed?

Bedside Manner

Some owners need a lot of hand holding and a welcoming staff when it comes to their dog's care, and that is absolutely fine. Unfortunately, vets are not always the most people-oriented people and their staff can be downright rude. One vet here in L.A. is absolutely wonderful with animals, but has been known to make clients cry. Another vet I work with has a scheduler who seems to derive a sick pleasure out of making clients wait on hold. While I have great confidence in both of these vets' medical skills, I would never recommend either to a novice dog owner. Instead, you should choose a vet who you trust and an office environment where you feel comfortable.

Availability

My vet is constantly slammed with appointments. While he does an amazing job of giving everyone a lot of attention, his waiting room can get very backed up and it can take a week or more to get in to see him (he will, of course, see you if there is an emergency). For some dog owners that's a no-go, and that's fine. But you should be suspicious if your vet office seems like a ghost town. Vet offices should be somewhat bustling.

Convenience/Hours

My vet recently decided to close on the weekends. While it works just fine for me—I work nearby, and have a flexible job—his limited hours have been prohibitive for other dog owners. Some vets have extended hours and even work on Sunday. Look around and don't feel bad if you must work convenience into your equation. Getting your dog to the vet on a yearly basis is important no matter what day of the week it happens.

Ultimately, you have to go with your gut when choosing a vet. Remember, you are the client and you have to be comfortable.

Lewis and Monkey

Never underestimate the power of bribery when it comes to providing food and drink to a vet's office staff, especially at a twenty-four-hour emergency vet hospital. My friend Lewis's dog, Monkey, had emergency surgery and had to be kept for a few days. Lewis religiously brought that staff coffee and donuts every night before he went to sleep. This simple act paved the way for him to go into a restricted area to give Monkey some much-needed TLC while he was hooked up to his IV. Moreover, the outlay Lewis made buying treats for the staff paid off. Many vet hospital fees can be discounted or omitted if the staff so chooses. Lewis's bill was significantly lower than it may have been otherwise. While the discount may or may not happen for you, the investment in getting the staff sweet on your dog will be well worth the extra ten bucks a day.

Preventative Measures

One of the most common concerns single owners have is the cost of caring for their dog. Vet bills can really mount up, even if you are cost conscious and conservative. While it is impossible to protect your dog 100 percent from getting sick, there are a few ways to keep your dog safer and more affordable.

Leashes Save Money and Lives

Always have your dog on a leash, but preferably not on one that's retractable. These plastic-handled leashes allow dogs to walk at an adjustable distance in front of their handler and can be dangerous. Dogs are ruled by instinct, and they don't know not to run into traffic after a squirrel or not to pick on the unruly dog that's eight times their size. If your dog is off leash or on too long of a lead, you have compromised your authority. When walking a dog, keep her firmly at your side. This cements your position as pack leader, and keeps her out of harm's way.

Food

Feed your dog high-quality food and stay consistent. Dogs are what they eat. If bad food goes in, chronic and costly veterinary problems may arise: skin allergies, ear infections, indigestion, and anal-gland issues. So while good food may cost more per bag, a dollar spent today may save you tenfold on vet care down the road.

While I would never suggest skimping on your dog's medical care, there are two places where you can save money in terms of vet care: vaccine clinics and spay/neuter clinics.

Vaccination Clinics

Vaccination clinics are offered at local shelters, pet stores like PETCO and PetSmart, and even some dog parks. These clinics provide the same vaccines available at your vet, but at a discounted rate. However, if you use a vaccination clinic, remember to keep a record of the vaccines given. Without records, you have no proof that your dog was properly vaccinated, and if you have to travel, board your dog, or renew your dog's license, you may have to repeat vaccinations.

Spay or Neuter Your Dog

Aside from the fact that the act of spaying or neutering will save you tons of money in the long run (a dog in heat will ruin your house; unfixed male dogs are more likely to engage in fights; having puppies, especially unexpected ones, is crazy-expensive), there are many low-cost spay/neuter outfits operating across the country. Some are for-profit clinics that focus solely on spay/neuter. Others are nonprofit groups who provide spay/neuter services at a discount or even free as a way to curb pet overpopulation. While you might not get the touchy-feely treatment you get at a full-service vet, for the most part, these low-cost options are safe.

The biggest drawback to these mobile and low-cost services is that they don't keep animals overnight. While overnight care isn't mandatory, complications do happen in a small percentage of the millions of spays and neuters done each year. So, do your homework and see what the aftercare services look like. In case of a problem, you can bring your dog to a twenty-four-hour clinic, but it's best if whatever service you use has an after-hours contact number or facility to handle post-surgical issues.

DOGMA:

Save Online!

Dog owners can save a lot of money by purchasing their dog's medications, flea control, and general supplies from online retailers such as Doctors Foster and Smith (*www.drsfostersmith.com*), Entirely Pets (*www.entirelypets.com*), and 1-800-PetMeds (*www.1800petmeds.com*). Discounts vary, but I have saved as much as 50 percent on meds, treats, and tools! To save even more, ask other dog owners to split an order with you. Greater discounts are often given if you buy in bulk!

Pet Insurance or Savings Account

I am a huge proponent of getting pet insurance. When Bella's spleen burst, the surgery that saved her life cost $2,300. Thankfully, I had purchased pet insurance six weeks beforehand. It was only a mid-level policy with a 70 percent payout—the total reimbursement after meeting the deductible and with follow-up visits was approximately $1,700. It is extremely common for dogs to be given up when they need costly treatment, a sad situation that could be avoided if a dog owner invested in a pet insurance policy.

Pet insurance isn't perfect, though. Dealing with insurance can be a full-time job. What will a carrier cover? Have you met your deductible? I have heard some stories that some carriers have denied coverage on lame technicalities, as too often happens with human insurance. Also, many pet insurance policies won't insure dogs of a certain breed against the diseases that most commonly affect them. Similarly, some carriers won't insure older dogs against any pre-existing conditions. An alternative plan is to create a savings account for your dog's health care. Put aside a certain amount in an account every month, in your mind or under your mattress if you must, to cover your vet costs. If you aren't the type to follow through, file claims, and stay on top of your dog's insurance policy, a pet-care savings account might be a good option. You can also augment your safety net by buying an accident-only policy for those unforeseen times when stuff just happens.

CANINE CONSIDERATION ❖ ❖ ❖

Protect your dog: Get pet insurance or start a pet savings account.

Unexpected Medical Issues

Even if you follow all the rules, unexpected things happen. Of course, the idea of your dog getting sick or injured is not something you want to think about, but even when an owner is vigilant and cares deeply for his pooch, accidents and illnesses can occur. Before you freak at the thought, stop and breathe.

Charles and Billie

You can get through a medical emergency just as my friend Charles did when his Bulldog, Billie, was attacked by two coyotes. Somehow, Charles and a family friend managed to scare off the coyotes, but Billie was riddled with puncture wounds.

Charles rushed Billie to the emergency vet hospital, hoping for the best but fearing the worst. Billie was in the hospital for close to three weeks, and Charles was beside himself. While he couldn't do much to help soothe Billie's significant physical injuries, Charles did everything he could to soothe Billie emotionally. He brought Billie's favorite blanket and stuffed animal, and every day he brought Billie the shirt he'd slept in the night before so Billie always felt his presence. Plus, Charles spent at least an hour every day just holding him.

Billie made it through this hellish ordeal with flying colors. I am sure that his recovery was due in no small part to the intense dedication Charles showed during his recovery. Remember, you are your dog's best and only advocate when they get sick. Your attention will not only help your dog heal, but your presence at the vet hospital will keep the staff's attention locked on your dog as well.

When your dog gets sick, don't just let things happen. While still being gracious, watch to make sure your dog is getting the care she needs and deserves.

Alternative Vet Care

Alternative or complementary veterinary care such as acupuncture, energy healing, or canine massage may seem New Age, indulgent, or even frivolous to some. To me, these treatments are lifesavers.

——————————————— **Tucker** ———————————————

Tucker, the dog I got in college who now lives with my parents, is a big fifteen-plus-year-old dog. For all intents and purposes, she has no business being the spry, couch-hopping, stair-climbing girl she is today. I credit her good health to Dr. Joann Boyer, a veterinary acupuncturist who has been treating Tucker for the last two years.

Dr. Joann started to treat Tucker after an X-ray showed what appeared to be a mass on her liver. A proper biopsy would require Tucker to be put under general anesthesia while the vet performed a somewhat invasive procedure. Although willing to do whatever it took to keep her healthy, at age thirteen, Tucker had already lived a long and wonderful life. Putting her through any of these painful treatments for what could have been a difference of only a few weeks or months would truly be for our benefit and not hers. Instead, I decided to manage her pain, allowing her to live out the rest of her life with belly rubs and kisses instead of trips to the vet, which she particularly hated.

Already hooked into the dog world, I knew dogs with everything from allergies to cancer that enjoyed great results with alternative veterinary medicine, particularly acupuncture. I figured alternative medicine might be a good fit for Tucker's situation. A veterinary acupuncturist could treat Tucker's ailments whether related to the mass or not, without putting her through any pain. In fact, Tucker loves her acupuncture treatments and absolutely adores Dr. Joann. Now, at first sight of her, Tucker high-tails it to my parent's room where she gets her treatments. Before signing your dog up for acupuncture, however, it's helpful to have a basic understanding of how acupuncture actually works.

What Is Veterinary Acupuncture and How Does It Work?

According to the American Veterinary Acupuncture Society, all disease is caused by an imbalance or disruption in the flow

DOGMA:

Dog Years

The average lifespan for American dogs is between ten and twelve years. Small-breed dogs such as Jack Russell Terriers tend to be about thirteen years old, while larger dogs such as Shepherds and Labradors only live to be around ten years old. Giant breeds such as Mastiffs and Bernese Mountain dogs have an even shorter lifespan, just eight to ten years.

of energy. From an Eastern medicine point of view, energy in the body flows through a system of channels or meridians. Trained practitioners can improve the flow of energy in the body by applying needles, heat, pressure (massage or acupressure), or one of a variety of new technologies such as lasers or electronic stimulation at certain prescribed points on the body. By improving energy flow, acupuncture may help bring an animal's energy back into balance, bringing the animal back to good health.

Think of a body like a Christmas tree. The meridians are like strings of Christmas lights, and each bulb along the string is a point along one of the meridians. If one bulb on the string is loose, the bulbs beyond that point go dark; energy can't flow through to those bulbs. If you screw in that bulb, the energy can flow again and all is well; you have a beautiful, vibrant tree. Acupuncture, placing the needle in a point where the energy is backed up, is just like screwing in that light bulb; it allows the energy to flow again along the meridians and good health to return.

▼ What Can You Expect in a Treatment?

Just like a trip to your regular vet, an acupuncture appointment starts with a careful examination of your dog from nose to tail. Using all of this information, as well as the information you provide detailing any changes in eating, behavioral, or bathroom habits, the acupuncturist can synthesize his treatment plan—where the needles will be placed and for how long, and if any herbal remedies will be prescribed. Then it's time for the needles.

I hate needles and shots as much as or more than anyone else; but seriously, acupuncture is relatively pain free. Acupuncture needles are incredibly thin and, while solid, are flexible and only penetrate the top layer of the skin. According to Dr. Joann, approximately 90 to 95 percent of her patients rest comfortably with the needles in place, and some dogs will even fall asleep during treatment.

However, if your dog isn't having such an easy time or she appears to be experiencing more than a moment of discomfort, don't push it and don't be shy. Communicate with the acupuncturist; express your concern calmly. Acupuncture may not be right for your dog, and that's fine. Making your dog uncomfortable, even if it's with the ultimate goal of helping her, is simply not worth it.

▼ How to Find a Good Acupuncturist

It is essential to choose a veterinary acupuncturist who is well trained, experienced, and most importantly, certified. Certification from a group such as International Veterinary Acupuncture Society (*www.ivas.org*) or the American Academy of Veterinary Acupuncture (*www.aava.org*) means the doctor has the necessary training and experience to properly treat your dog. Be careful; just because someone took a course does not mean they are certified. Seminars are available to both veterinarians and human acupuncturists alike, but certification is a far more extensive process. While important to educate people about the benefits of veterinary acupuncture, these courses, even for a vet with years of Western-style veterinary education and treatment experience, do not make for sufficient acupuncture training. Vets may have a command of canine anatomy and medicine, but their lack of familiarity with energy points, needle placement, and herbs could be extremely dangerous for your dog. Similarly, human acupuncturists may have vast experience and skill with acupuncture, but their insufficient knowledge of canine anatomy and diseases combined with a lack of experience treating patients who can't talk, and might bite, could produce big problems as well.

If you aren't near an alternative vet, contact the one closest to you and see if they can refer you to a practitioner who might be certified through another organization or who practices a different form of alternative healing such as canine massage or energy healing.

Herbs

An important component of alternative or complementary medicine for people as well as for animals is the use of herbs. While a big proponent of herbal medicine, I draw the line at unsupervised, over-the-counter herb use. Sounds a little dramatic, but I'm beyond serious. Herbal remedies can be just as powerful as any medication a traditional vet would prescribe for your dog and should be administered with the same, if not more, care and attention.

DOGMA:

Balancing Act

Energy healing is based on the notion that during periods of emotional distress or physical disease energy within the body as well as the energy fields that surround the body become unbalanced. Energy healers utilize various techniques such as Reiki, sound therapy, and massage to bring energy back into balance.

As always, I speak on this topic from painful experience. While living in Seattle, the training facility Bella almost flunked out of (due to separation anxiety) recommended an herbalist to prescribe her a calming remedy. I had a brief conversation with the herbalist and told her what was going on with Bella. Three days later a package of herbs arrived in the mail. They were in baggies not bottles, and were labeled with the name of the remedy and how many Bella should get each day. That should have been my first clue something was amiss, but figuring the training facility, known as the best in the region, would only recommend a trustworthy herbalist, I started Bella on the herbs.

While I can't squarely blame what happened next on the herbs, I believe they played a part. Soon after, Bella started vomiting, which continued through weeks of intermittent diarrhea and listlessness. After two emergency surgeries, and a vet bill equal to a down payment on a condo, Bella eventually regained her health and I my sanity. But the process most likely could have been avoided had I been more careful about the herbs.

Certainly, a dog may have a bad reaction to veterinarian-prescribed medications, but these drugs are regulated and consistent. Herbs and herbal remedies are not. I knew the names of some of the herbs Bella was taking, but had no idea what their strength was or how concentrated they were. To make matters worse, the herbalist was on vacation in China and couldn't be reached. So, while I am not trying to discourage you from giving your dogs herbs, I strongly encourage you to do so under the close supervision of an experienced—and reachable—doctor or licensed herbalist.

Massage, Chiropractic, and Physical Therapies

There are many other complementary therapies in addition to acupuncture and herbs, such as canine massage, chiropractic care, and physical therapy, which can significantly improve a dog's health and vitality. Marlene Grass, RVT, CMT, writes in an article for Petplace.com, that the soothing sensation of touch and the manipulation of muscles may provide benefits for dogs including:

- An increased overall sense of wellness
- A general sense of calming and reduction of stress
- Increased flexibility and movement
- Pain reduction or relief of pain
- Decreased recovery time from surgery or trauma
- Increased circulation of the blood, lymphatic, and nervous systems
- Removal of toxins from the body and its organs

Independent practitioners as well as doggie spas with services such as water therapy, massage, and assisted exercise have opened shop across the country. These treatments can be

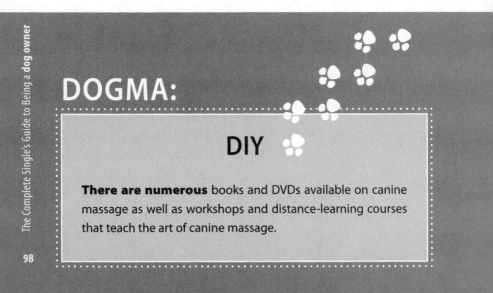

DOGMA:

DIY

There are numerous books and DVDs available on canine massage as well as workshops and distance-learning courses that teach the art of canine massage.

tremendously helpful for dogs dealing with the above problems. But again, as with acupuncture and herbs, check the credentials of anyone who lays their hands on your dog.

Finally, remember that dogs take cues from their owners; if you don't feel comfortable with the person giving your dog acupuncture, massage, herbs, or energy work, chances are your dog won't either.

CANINE CONSIDERATION ❖ ❖ ❖

Remember, whatever health-care option you choose for your dog, you both need to feel comfortable. Choose a vet that you trust and, if you're even the slightest bit open to alternative therapies, give them a try. They do work and may save you money and, more importantly, the heartache of seeing your dog experience avoidable pain, such as that caused by arthritis or a slipped disk!

it's a dog's life:
beyond fleas and ticks

There are so many health-related issues to think about when getting a dog that trying to wrap your mind around them can be intimidating—especially for a single person. So, before you get overwhelmed, stop and check out this list of pertinent veterinary issues—there are quite a few, but it's manageable . . . I promise!

Flea and Tick Prevention

Part of having a healthy dog is having a cootie-free dog. Fleas and ticks aren't just gross; they can be dangerous to your dog's health. Technically speaking, these vile little critters are parasites and, if they're hanging out on your dog, they are literally sucking your dog's blood. Thankfully, we have come a long way from those useless flea collars of old. Products like K9 Advantage and Frontline are topical treatments that you apply to the nape of your dog's neck. The ointments are absorbed into the bloodstream and make it possible for dogs to repel fleas and ticks and the diseases they bring.

Vaccines

Whether bringing home a puppy or an adult dog, there are a few basic dog health issues to get squared away, and first on the list are vaccines. Different areas of the country see different canine

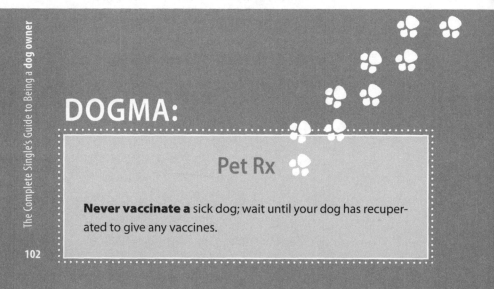

DOGMA:

Pet Rx

Never vaccinate a sick dog; wait until your dog has recuperated to give any vaccines.

diseases, so vaccination protocols will vary from state to state. Commonly, dogs are given what's known as a DHLPP—one injection to protect them against five nasty diseases, also known as a five-in-one shot. Included are vaccines to prevent against the following:

D—Distemper, a deadly disease
H—Hepatitis, a very contagious disease that attacks a dog's organs
L—Leptospiros, a life-threatening disease that dogs get through contact with the urine of an infected host
P—Parvovirus or parvo, a viral infection most common in puppies and young dogs
P—Para-influenza, a highly contagious upper-respiratory disease

To be sure your dog is protected, check with your vet or local animal shelter to see what vaccines are needed for your area and any area to which you travel on a regular basis. It is perfectly acceptable for your veterinarian to split up the shots. And if a disease is not present in your area, skip that vaccine. It's best not to overstress your dog's system with unnecessary inoculations.

Adult dogs who are being vaccinated for the first time should be good to go with a single round of shots followed by annual boosters, but puppy shots must be repeated three times between six and eighteen weeks of age to catch that window when the mother's antibodies from nursing wear off and the pup's kick in. Until a pup has had a full course of shots, avoid dog parks where he may come into contact with unvaccinated dogs or puppies. Don't think your dog is safe just because the other dogs seem fine. A dog can be asymptomatic and still spread that disease to other dogs.

While having your puppy fully vaccinated is a must, there is some credible questioning in the veterinary community about the need for vaccinating older, previously well-vaccinated dogs. The immunity in their systems from earlier vaccines may be sufficient and they may not need to get yearly boosters. The jury is still out, so consult your vet. But no matter what your vet says about booster shots, there are two core vaccines that all dogs must have: bordetella and rabies.

CANINE CONSIDERATION ❖ ❖ ❖

Vaccinate your dog and be sure to keep those vaccines up to date. Also, keep a record in your files.

Bordetella

Getting your dog a bordetella vaccine is like getting yourself a flu shot. Bordetella is more commonly known as kennel cough. Although it may sound like something you can skip, you can't. A bordetella vaccination can be given as early as six to eight weeks of age and, especially for the single owner, is essential because you cannot board a dog without this particular vaccine being up to date. Many day cares and kennels require a dog to have been vaccinated within the last six months, but no less than ten days before boarding (as the vaccine takes a few days to kick in). This may not sound like such a big deal, but far too many times friends have called me in a panic because they need to get their dog vaccinated ASAP so they can board them due to a last-minute trip.

Rabies

Rabies is another important vaccine that may be hard to understand. After all, how common are rabid dogs these days?

Thankfully, not common at all, due to widespread vaccination. Again, your dog probably won't be getting rabies, but rabies vaccines are required by law in every state for licensing your dog. If, God forbid, your dog bites someone and you don't have proof of vaccination, you'll be putting your dog's life at risk because the authorities may insist on quarantining your dog, or worse, euthanizing her. This is an avoidable problem if you just remember to get your dog's rabies shots on a regular basis.

Vaccination clinics can be found in most cities—especially on the weekends—at vet hospitals, PETCO, PetSmart, and local shelters. These clinics offer the same vaccines as your vet, but at reduced prices. To find a clinic in your area, try *www.petservice.com*, then click "Vaccination Clinics," or simply use Google and enter "vaccination clinic" and your zip code. One caveat, though: Vaccine clinics are not full-service vets. So, if you use a clinic, be sure to bring a copy of the shot records with you to your regular vet so you can keep your dog's file up to date.

Spay/Neuter

Spaying refers to removing a female dog's reproductive organs and neutering refers to removing a male dog's reproductive organs (his testicles). Don't feel stupid if you didn't know this—people often get confused!

Many new owners ask me if they really need to spay or neuter their dog. The answer from trusted organizations such as the American Humane Society and the American Veterinary Medical association is a resounding, "YES!!!" Fixing your dog is necessary and beneficial to you, your pet, and the world at large. Above and beyond animal overpopulation issues (there are simply too many puppies born to give them all homes, resulting in 4–6 million pets being euthanized each year in America alone), there are health benefits to fixing your pet. Spay and neuter surgeries are routine and safe. Dogs can be altered at almost any age, but it is better to have the surgery done when a dog is young. Cost depends on where you live and how big your dog is. Rule of thumb: The bigger the dog the bigger the bill. Super-tiny dogs are an exception because of their delicate nature.

Due to the focus on stopping pet overpopulation, low-cost spay/neuter programs are popping up around the country. Organizations such as SNAP (Spay Neuter Assistance Program) have programs providing free or low-cost spay/neuter programs. There are currently programs running in Texas, Louisiana, New Mexico, and California among other states. Similarly, the North Shore Animal League has a site at *www.spayusa.org* to help you find programs in your area.

DOGMA:

Pest Control

It's a myth that dogs only need flea and tick protection in the summer. Dogs need flea and tick protection year round!

CANINE CONSIDERATION ❖ ❖ ❖

The benefits of spaying or neutering your pet far outweigh any drawbacks.

Female Dogs

There is a longstanding myth that it's advantageous for a female dog to go into heat once before spaying her. Instead, spaying your dog before she goes into heat allows her to avoid mammary cancer later in life as well as other unpleasant diseases such as pyometra, a painful disease of the uterus common in unfixed older, female dogs.

In addition to health advantages, there are major lifestyle benefits to having a dog spayed in advance of her first heat; namely, not having to deal with a dog in heat! The term "like a bitch in heat" couldn't be more accurate. The phrase "going into heat" essentially means your dog has her period for twenty-one days, during which time she will pee in undesirable places, cover your walls and floors with blood, and become anxious and short tempered. She will also be actively seeking a dog with whom she can mate. And, while she's on the prowl for some action, male dogs from as far away as two city blocks will be looking for her. You must keep a dog in heat safely away from other dogs not just to avoid unwanted pregnancy, but to avoid fights that can occur as a result of the hormonally charged interactions a dog in heat can trigger.

There is also the misconception that a dog should have a litter of puppies before she is spayed. This is an even bigger myth, and the consequences can be overwhelming. The idea of a litter from a beloved dog is enticing, but the reality is anything but. One trip to the shelter to see all the unwanted puppies should show you that there are enough puppies in the world. If that doesn't convince you, know that raising a litter of pups is challenging, dirty, often heartbreaking, work.

Male Dogs

With male dogs, the consequence might not be as burdensome as ending up with a litter of unwanted puppies, but the reasons to neuter are still quite convincing. Once an unneutered dog reaches maturity, at six to nine months depending on the breed, he will likely begin marking his territory—peeing on just about anything in his path. It's an instinctual behavior telling other dogs, "This is my turf!" This behavior is difficult to break, as is an unfixed male dog's instinct to take off from home in search of a female with whom to rendezvous. Sadly, in their search for love, many of these dogs end up lost or hit by cars.

An unfixed male dog can also become aggressive. An intact male will fight with other dogs for first dibs on a female, possibly injuring himself, other dogs, and people. In fact, unaltered dogs

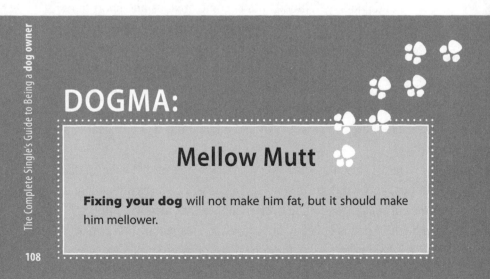

DOGMA:

Mellow Mutt

Fixing your dog will not make him fat, but it should make him mellower.

are three times more likely to attack humans and other animals. Health-wise, neutering a dog will prevent debilitating and common diseases later in life such as prostate and testicular cancer.

Serious, or Seriously Neurotic?

As an owner, you are the gatekeeper for your dog's health, responsible for basic health care such as making sure your dog is fixed and up to date on shots as well as in more complex situations where you need to make a judgment call on whether your dog needs to go to the vet. Your dog can't tell you how bad she feels or point to where it hurts, and finding out what's wrong often requires a vet visit.

Not all illnesses present themselves with obvious or pronounced symptoms. A good owner must watch out for generalized symptoms as well. The first questions a vet will ask are to get a sense of whether anything has changed in your dog's general well-being. How is her energy level? Have her eating, drinking, or bathroom habits changed recently? Is she restless or pacing? Is she lethargic?

Pay attention to what's going on with your dog. Even the best vet will rely on a dog's owner to provide a sense of how your dog's current state compares to her normal state.

Keep in mind your dog's eating, drinking, and bathroom habits as well as her energy level. Changes in these can indicate bigger issues and you will be the only one to provide your vet with this information. And you can forget the wet-nose test. Checking to see if your dog's nose is wet or dry won't be a true indication of her health. If you want to be extra on top of tracking your dog's health, though, you could get a thermometer (get the kind that goes in her ear, not her tush). Get a baseline temperature when your dog is healthy (normal temperature range is between 100.5°F and 102.5°F, but every dog will be different); then when you're concerned that she isn't well, you will have something to compare it to.

Common Doggie Ailments Decoded

There are millions of scenarios in which your dog will need to go to a vet, but here are a few common ailments, how to spot them, and what you can do to avoid them.

Gastric Disorders

The most common ailments that bring dogs to the vet are gastric issues or stomach upset, symptoms of which include vomiting, diarrhea, and the ever-pleasant butt scoot.

DOGMA:

Vet Vibe

Don't expect the warm fuzzies from ER vets. Twenty-four-hour emergency hospitals are there to stabilize your dog, not be your best friend. Also, just like when you end up in the emergency room, ER vets will often charge first and ask questions later; plus, interns usually staff these facilities. So, if at all possible, ask that the ER stabilize your dog then bring her to your own vet—with whom you have, hopefully, developed a strong rapport—as soon as possible.

▼ How Do Dogs Get It?

Dogs will develop stomach problems from a variety of sources. Just as people get food poisoning or the stomach flu, your dog's stomach issues will most likely be from either something he ate or from a bacterial infection he picked up on the street or at the dog park.

▼ Prevention

The best way to avoid stomach problems is to keep your dog's food consistent. Table scraps, steak, or sausage off the grill, random dog treats, or extra-rich dog treats can all set off a gastric episode. More serious issues can be contagious and are passed from dog to dog. Avoiding the dog park may be a good way to keep your dog's stomach on track.

DOGMA:

Down Dogs

Lethargy is a state of drowsiness, inactivity, or indifference in which there are delayed responses to external stimuli such as auditory (sound), visual (sight), or tactile (touch) stimuli. Lethargy may also refer to the general malaise and decreased activity exhibited by animals that do not feel well.

If you're not sure whether your dog's upset stomach is a consequence of table scraps or a contagious illness, it's a good idea to keep him sequestered from other dogs until things pass or you receive a diagnosis from your vet. If you have more than one dog, chances are they've shared whatever cooties they may have before you're even aware there's a problem, so you'll want to watch both of them closely. Also, be sure to keep all your dogs, sick or well, away from feces—a common way illnesses are passed from dog to dog.

▼ Treatment

Your vet can prescribe medications to soothe your dog's intestinal tract and slow down diarrhea and vomiting, but there are some things you can do at home to help her feel better. I call them the three Ps: plain food, pumpkin, and Pepcid.

Plain food such as steamed chicken, plain rice, cottage cheese, and chicken broth will help calm your dog's stomach and allow

DOGMA:

Pop a Pill

Make giving your dog his meds as painless as possible by hiding all pills in hunks of cheese, peanut butter, lunch meat, or using Pill Pockets. Pill Pockets, bite-sized pill holders made of dog food, are a genius product available at most pet stores. You just pop your dog's pill inside, mush, and serve!

her to recuperate more easily. Similarly, adding canned pumpkin (not pumpkin-pie filling) to your dog's food will soothe her lower intestinal tract to help alleviate symptoms of diarrhea. Also, just as you might reach for the antacid when you have indigestion, giving your dog a product such as Pepcid will alleviate a number of stomach ailments. However, it is important to remember that Pepcid is still a drug, and it's important to check with your vet for dosage and drug interaction.

▼ How Serious?

The hardest part of having a dog with stomach issues—especially for new owners—is not knowing if these are symptoms of something bigger or are simply a passing problem.

For the most part this will be a short-lived stomach issue—something akin to you getting indigestion after eating food that didn't agree with you. But how do you know? The best way to assess your dog's tummy status is to wait a few hours and let him relax—don't feed him, don't stimulate him. Then, after a few hours have passed, offer him food and water in small amounts. If the dog is bright and alert and wants to eat, he should probably be fine. If things persist, particularly for more than twenty-four hours, or if your dog's stomach distress is ever combined with a state of lethargy, be sure to take him to the vet ASAP.

Kennel Cough

Kennel cough, also known as bordetella, is a bronchial condition characterized by a hacking cough.

▼ How Do Dogs Get It?

Due to the highly contagious nature of kennel cough, dogs most commonly get sick when they have been with other dogs.

But kennels aren't the only place a dog can get sick; dog parks, shelters, the vet, and doggie day cares are also havens for kennel cough.

▼ Prevention

The bordetella vaccine that your dog gets should help protect her against kennel cough, but it is possible for her to get an alternative strain even if fully vaccinated.

▼ Treatment

Some vets won't even prescribe medication for kennel cough, while others will give your dog a cough suppressant. Either way, you will need to watch that it doesn't progress beyond the cough.

▼ How Serious?

It sounds awful and, while it's painful to watch your dog wheeze as though something is stuck in his throat, kennel cough by itself is not that grave. It's about as serious as people getting a chest cold. However, if your dog's cough persists or it is accompanied by nasal discharge—particularly if it's yellow or green—it is imperative that you contact your vet immediately. The presence of nasal discharge or any lethargy could be indicative of much bigger problems, especially in puppies.

Skin Issues (Mange)

There are two different kinds of mange that cause your dog to lose her hair: sarcoptic, which is contagious, and demodectic (demodex), which is not.

▼ How Do Dogs Get It?

According to veterinarian Dr. Race Foster, demodex is "generally a disease of young dogs that have inadequate or poorly developed immune systems or older dogs that are suffering from a depressed immune system." Dogs and people alike have little mites living on their skin at all times, but a dog with a compromised immune system can't keep the mites under control and they multiply, eating away at your dog's coat. In puppies, the condition is usually passed down from a mom to her pup and in adult dogs the condition can be set off by trauma, nerves, or a nutritive deficiency.

Sarcoptic mange is otherwise known as canine scabies. These microscopic mites invade the skin of healthy dogs or puppies and create a variety of skin problems, the most common of which is hair loss and severe itching. Dogs come into contact with these mites in the same places they come into contact with kennel cough—grooming facilities, dog parks, shelters, doggie day cares, and kennels.

▼ Prevention

The best way to protect your dog from both kinds of mange is to keep his immune system strong with good food and nutritional supplements, and by keeping him away from places where dogs you don't know the health of congregate. You can also give your dog Revolution, an amazing medication. You place a monthly, small tube-full on the back of your dog's neck and it goes in through his skin, not only preventing and controlling sarcoptic mange, but preventing heartworm disease, controlling some intestinal parasites, killing fleas, and stopping flea eggs from hatching.

it's a dog's life: beyond fleas and ticks

▼ Treatment

Treating mange is not fun. Both varieties can be persistent and challenging to beat. Your vet will most likely prescribe oral medications, but you'll also have to bring your dog in for powerful weekly treatments known as dips, which kill the mites on your dog's skin, but also really stink.

▼ How Serious?

While neither version of mange is life-threatening, both are awful and uncomfortable for the dog and can be painful for you to handle. Sarcoptic mange, while highly contagious to people and other animals, is far easier to get rid of, while demodex tends to be difficult to shake.

Due to the contagious nature of sarcoptic mange, you'll want to keep your dog away from other dogs, even those in the same home. Be sure to scrub down your home to get rid of any mites, treat any other dogs in the house with Revolution, and wash all sheets thoroughly.

Periodontal Disease

Bad dog breath isn't quite as innocuous as you may think. If a dog's breath smells particularly foul, there is a good chance your dog has gum disease. Beyond the repulsive smell lurk some serious health risks. That yellowy tartar buildup on your dog's teeth can lead to heart disease and tooth loss.

▼ How Do Dogs Get It?

A dog doesn't have to be neglected for dental disease to get out of control. Tartar builds on your dog's teeth just as it does on human teeth, and some smaller breeds (Maltese, Poodles, and Pekingese) are more prone to dental disease than others. For these breeds and for those who have not taken the preventative measures, there is little you can do other than taking your dog in for regular teeth cleaning.

▼ Prevention

The key to good oral health in dogs is plaque-free teeth. To achieve this goal, the Veterinary Oral Health Council (*www.vohc.org*) recommends that a dog engage in "daily chewing" activity. A dog should eat at least some dry food every day and or have a treat or bone to help scrape away tartar. The council also advocates brushing your dog's teeth on a regular basis and bringing them in for annual or even biannual cleanings. Some dogs might not need such regular cleanings, but if your dog has any of that yellowy-brown stuff building, if any teeth are loose, or if your dog shows any mouth sensitivity, it's best to consult your vet about a dental cleaning and potentially a set of dental X-rays just to be sure bigger problems have not developed.

▼ Treatment

A hot topic in doggie dental circles is anesthesia-free cleaning. The results are comparable to traditional teeth cleanings, and it's always nice not to have to put your dog under anesthesia unnecessarily. However, many argue that a dog's teeth should only be cleaned under anesthesia and under the care of a board-certified vet. This is one of those decisions that you will have to make for yourself. Whichever way you choose, treatments can range from routine to aggressive, but sometimes decay has progressed too far and a dog's teeth have to be removed. While quite sad for a dog to lose teeth, rotten teeth hurt, and removing a diseased tooth can give a previously sad or depressed dog a whole new joie de vivre.

The truth is, most people don't realize how dangerous that brown plaque is until it's too late. Aside from dental disease affecting a dog's mouth, bad teeth can lead to kidney, liver, heart, and joint disease because the bacteria can end up in your dog's bloodstream.

Joy and Nappy

Joy adopted a sweet elderly terrier named Napoleon. When Joy got Nappy, his mouth was full of brown, rotten teeth, and while she debated whether to have them removed—different vets had different opinions—Nappy developed an infection that ate a hole through his throat. Joy had no choice but to take out all of his teeth immediately. After his procedure, Nappy had two and half teeth left, but he felt like a king. His infection was gone, his breath was better, and true to his amazing spirit, Nappy still ate kibble like it was cotton candy. Not all dogs are as lucky as Nappy, so be sure to pay attention to your dog's dental health.

diet and exercise for your dog

As if it's not hard enough to manage your own eating and fitness habits, when you have a dog you're also responsible for their diet and exercise. It's as easy to feed a dog cheap food and table scraps as it is for you to grab that slice of pizza for dinner—but are these options healthy? Of course not! You deserve better . . . and so does your dog!

Dog Diets

Part of keeping a dog healthy is feeding her a healthy diet. Unfortunately, all pet food is not created equal. Many mainstream brands use low-quality meats, funky preservatives, and ingredients you would be somewhat horrified to know about. Suffice it to say, that pet food isn't regulated to the same standards as people food. Hopefully this will change, but in the meantime you can make sure your dog stays healthy by feeding her high-quality food. This doesn't mean you have to start cooking for your dog on a full-time basis or get a second job so you can afford an all-organic diet, but it does mean you need to pay a little more per bag.

No matter how much you're willing to spend, the choices can be a little confusing. Wet or dry? Your vet sells one brand of food. Your breeder or rescue group tells you another and then some people swear by the raw diet. It's enough to make you crazy. Unfortunately, while I can't give you a definitive answer on one perfect dog diet that will work for all dogs all the time, I can give you a better understanding of your options so you can make the right decision for your dog.

CANINE CONSIDERATION ❖ ❖ ❖

The saying "You are what you eat" holds just as true for your dog as it does for you.

Wet Versus Dry

A common misconception is that feeding your dog wet food is always better than feeding him kibble. Although it's hard to think of those little brown pellets of dry dog food as nutritious or appealing, this thinking is somewhat backward. Dry food has many benefits, health and otherwise.

While you want your dog to enjoy his meal, choosing a food over another based on how sumptuous you think it looks does your dog a disservice. Sure, that saucy, gooey wet food may be more tantalizing to your pup's taste buds, but your dog would also eat poop if given the opportunity. You need to make the decisions about his health because he obviously can't. Also, although nutritive value will vary across brands, dry food is often more nourishing than wet in terms of straight nutritional content.

Dry food is also far better for your dog's dental health. Wet food does nothing to strengthen a dog's teeth, but crunching on kibble will keep teeth strong and tartar free, while also protecting against heart disease and serious infection.

Dry food is also easier to deal with than wet food—and a better option for someone on the dating scene. Wet food has a fierce stench that can permeate your apartment or house, and generates tons of cans that you must throw away or recycle, which is not good for the environment or for taking out the trash—something I loathe doing! The residue wet food leaves behind on your dog's bowl will also mean that you'll have more dishes to wash, which is never a good thing.

CANINE CONSIDERATION ❖ ❖ ❖

Give your dog at least some dry food at every meal to help keep his teeth strong and clean.

Picking a Good Food (Wet or Dry)

Although dogs have evolved a great deal since their wild wolf days, their digestive systems have not. Keeping them on a diet rich in protein and low in grains or fillers is essential to keeping them healthy and allergy free.

Unfortunately, many commercial brands have it backwards and load their dog food—both wet and dry—with ingredients dogs just don't need like wheat, corn, and manmade fillers. These ingredients are cheap and make your dog feel full, but they do nothing nutritionally. Therefore, it's best to stick with foods the labels of which list a real protein source (such as chicken, lamb, or fish) as their first ingredient; ingredients are listed in order of weight.

While an entire book could be written about the particulars of choosing a dog food, keep the following in mind:

- A protein source should come first in the list of ingredients (unless your vet prescribes otherwise).
- Avoid food with ingredients you don't recognize.
- Be careful if there are numerous kinds of grains or glutens listed. This gives a protein source first billing, but allows

DOGMA:

Diet Details

Vegetarian owners might not like this, but dogs are carnivores and must have a meat-based diet. Unless your veterinarian prescribes a low-protein diet, depriving a dog of meat can seriously undermine her health.

less-expensive grain ingredients like wheat or corn to be the majority of the food.

- Cheap pet food is just that—cheap. It undermines your dog's health and can actually cost more in the long run because your dog will eat less food when you feed her food that's healthy and nutritionally dense.

CANINE CONSIDERATION ❖ ❖ ❖

All dog food is not created equal. Be wary when choosing a brand of dog food; the money you spend on a higher-quality brand will save you money in the long run.

Raw Diet

Raw diets have become quite the fad in the dog-food world. The basic premise of the raw diet is to feed your dog what she would have eaten as a wolf in the wild. While there are many versions of the raw diet, the most popular is the aptly named BARF Diet (Biologically Appropriate Raw Food or, as I call it, the Bones And Raw Food diet). Roughly, this diet entails feeding your dog whole meat including the bone, turkey or chicken necks, whole fish, or even rabbits. While for many a disgusting alternative to processed foods, it is also an extremely healthy approach for a dog, because a raw diet avoids the enormous amount of grain product found in commercial dog food.

However, while the raw diet could help prevent your dog from getting ill, it could cause some problems for you. Dogs can actually process a lot of bacteria present in raw meat, like E. coli and salmonella, that can make humans ill. So, if you want to prepare a raw-food diet for your dog, you're going to have to be super careful in terms of hygiene.

If you want to go raw and the idea of forking over raw meat to your dog on a regular basis seems overwhelming, you can purchase prepackaged raw food at most pet stores and healthy grocery-store chains such as Whole Foods. You still have to be careful with this prepackaged food in terms of cross-contamination and make sure your dog's bowl is well cleaned between meals, but because it's already cut into portions, there is far less work and less potential for illness.

Many critics of the BARF diet argue that it doesn't provide the essential vitamins needed to keep dogs healthy. So, if you're interested in the raw diet, don't just start feeding your dog steak or hamburger patties and call it a day. You must consult websites such as *www.barfworld.com* or, better yet, consult your vet about how to go about starting your pooch on the raw plan.

CANINE CONSIDERATION ❖ ❖ ❖

A properly balanced raw diet can do wonders for your dog's health. Just be sure you're on a prescribed plan and that you protect yourself against cross-contamination.

Prescription Dog Food

While I have laid out some good information on choosing a high-quality dog food, if you have a dog with a diagnosed illness, you may have to ignore everything I have just written.

Some dogs have conditions that would be exacerbated by a high-protein or raw-food diet. Bella, for instance, can't eat any of these foods because of a condition called Inflammatory Bowel

Syndrome. While I'd love to feed her a more natural diet, feeding her a scientifically formulated food has allowed her to lead a long and healthy life.

Ask your vet for her opinion on food, and follow her advice. Remember, any money you save now on food may be spent later treating chronic ear infections, cancer, or other illnesses.

CANINE CONSIDERATION ❖ ❖ ❖

If your dog has a health condition, talk to your doctor about food options that will help her feel better and get better.

Treats

Like choosing a food, choosing the right treat is essential. It doesn't make sense to feed your dog a high-quality food, just to undermine his health with gluten-filled dog treats. A good way to go is to stick with the treats made by the high-quality brand that makes your dog food. Otherwise, you lose the benefits of healthy foods once you introduce the preservatives, grease, and crap in a low-quality bag of treats.

Treats, however, can present more problems than just their ingredients. Chew treats, in particular, can be dangerous if your dog swallows them whole or swallows too large of a piece. In 2006, numerous dogs ingested large pieces of a popular brand of chew treats. Some dogs were able to handle the undigested treat—it came out the other end—but for others the treat caused an obstruction of their intestinal tract and the dogs died as a result. To avoid this kind of situation, choose appropriately sized treats for the size of your dog and keep a close eye on how ambitiously your dog devours his treat. Some dogs will work on a chew toy for hours, taking appropriate-size pieces while others, like Bella, tear through most in a hot second.

CANINE CONSIDERATION ❖ ❖ ❖

Watch how your dog handles a new treat. If he eats too much of the treat at one time or attempts to swallow it whole, take it from him immediately.

Some dog treats are just too rich and will upset more sensitive dogs' stomachs. While dog food is formulated to be easy to digest on a regular basis, treats should only be given in small amounts; and even then, they can be just too rich for some dogs to handle. Stay away from anything deep fried or overly greasy such as smoked knuckle bones or pigs' ears unless you know your dog has an iron stomach.

While every dog will be different, here are some great dog treats that most dogs should be able to enjoy safely.

▼ Bully Sticks

Bully sticks, also known as bull pizzle, are made from dried bull's penis. While there is something rather disturbing about your dog gnawing on a penis, dogs adore bully sticks. They can be too rich for some dogs, but because they are pure beef, they're 100 percent digestible. Like any treat, though, be sure to get the appropriate size bully stick so your dog doesn't swallow one whole.

▼ Marrow Bones

The biggest danger when giving a dog a bone is that it will splinter or fracture. This is why you should never give a dog cooked chicken, as cooked chicken bones are as sharp as needles. On the other hand, marrow bones are beef and therefore hearty and tough enough that your dog won't be able to swallow or splinter them.

However, finding true marrow bones can be challenging. Pet stores sell modified marrow bones alongside other chew treats, but these are disappointing compared to the real ones. The best marrow bones will be available in the freezer section of your pet store or from the butcher. Specialty grocery stores may carry marrow bones on a regular basis, but if you don't have one nearby, check with your local butcher. If they look at you like you're crazy, ask if they have a beef femur bone that can be cut into smaller sections.

Once you get home, keep the bones frozen and give them to your dog raw (you might want to let them thaw out a bit first). If the raw thing freaks you out, you can always cook the bones by roasting or boiling them. Also, if your dog is one to linger with her treats, it's best to limit her time with a raw bone. While dogs do have strong enzymes to kill off bacteria, it's just a bad idea to leave raw bones lying around for too long.

▼ Rawhides

Many people feel that rawhides are dangerous because they are not 100 percent digestible and have the potential to cause blockages. However, if rawhides are given in moderation, your dog should be able to enjoy them and not risk an obstruction. Rawhides provide a good distraction for dogs and best of all, you can find them almost anywhere.

▼ Kongs

While Kongs themselves are not treats, they provide an excellent treat-delivery system. These hard-rubber toys are incredibly durable and dogs go insane trying to get food, treats, and even peanut butter out of them. Plus, Kongs bounce if dropped, so your dog has to keep mentally focused in order to get his sweet reward. Kongs are great to give your dog when you head out or even if you need to keep them distracted while you are busy at home. They provide hours of entertainment, keeping your dog away from shoes, table legs, and counters.

▼ Antlerz (The Eco-Dog Treat)

Antlerz aren't quite as well known as the other treats and chews mentioned, but they are awesome. Wild deer shed their antlers once a year and then naturally regrow them. A Texas-based company recognized that the shed antlers provided the ultimate eco-friendly sustainable dog treat because these treats don't have to be farmed. Plus, they're really good for your dog. They don't require cooking, they're rich in minerals, and best of all dogs love them. Instead of biting off pieces, dogs slowly grind Antlerz down. This gives dogs' teeth a much-needed workout without ingesting the chemicals sometimes present in other dog chews. Antlerz come in tons of sizes. If your local store doesn't have them, find them online. It's good for the environment and good for your dog.

▼ Homemade Treats

If so motivated, you can always cook for your dog. There are entire dog cookbooks as well as numerous websites with fabulous dog recipes. Amy, my rescue partner, cooks for her dogs on a regular basis and they can't get enough of her homemade treats. Here is her favorite recipe for **Tank's Treats**:

tank's treats

Serving Size: 1–2 treats per day, or in line with what you would normally give your dog

For the liver:
½ pound calf liver (beef is fine)
1 tablespoon olive oil
2 bacon strips

For the treats:
1¼ cup flour
¾ cup soy flour
½ teaspoon salt
1¼ cup shredded Cheddar cheese
¼ teaspoon garlic powder
4–5 heaping tablespoons applesauce
2 tablespoons olive oil
3 heaping tablespoons liver mixture
4–5 tablespoons water (as needed)

1. Start by adding 1 tablespoon of olive oil to a pan.
2. Add bacon and liver.
3. Cook bacon until crispy; remove.
4. Cook liver on both sides until done; remove to a dish and cool.
5. Put bacon, liver, and the other tablespoon of olive oil in a food processor. Process until smooth (it should have the consistency of pate).
6. Mix the dry ingredients together in a bowl; set aside.
7. Mix together cheese, garlic, applesauce, olive oil, and liver mixture. Blend well with a spatula.
8. Add dry ingredients and mix well. If too dry, add water, a tablespoon at a time, until the mixture is moist.
9. Form into a ball and wrap in plastic. Refrigerate until cold.
10. Remove from fridge, put on lightly floured surface, and roll out to ½-inch thickness.
11. Cut shapes with cookie cutters.
12. Bake on lightly greased pan at 400°F for about 10 minutes, or until firm.

Dogs love these treats and they're healthier than anything you could buy at the store! This may seem painfully obvious, but when cooking for a dog, remember, the blander the better: boiled rice, boiled chicken, and maybe sweet potatoes should soothe your dog's stomach and make him feel loved.

CANINE CONSIDERATION ❖ ❖ ❖

Cooking for your dog shows how much you care. However, be careful to avoid giving a dog anything that is spiced or high in fat.

Dog Parks—Reality, Rules, and Etiquette

For urban and suburban owners, dog parks are not just a fun or social diversion, they are a necessity, providing dogs with the unparalleled opportunity to run and play freely. Respected dog trainer Brandan Fouche, in fact, encourages owners to incorporate dog-park trips into their routine because navigating the intricate process of pack dynamics—interacting with their canine "peers"—stimulates a dog both mentally and physically.

Unfortunately, not all dogs are cut out for the dog park, and that's okay. If your dog is aggressive or overly fearful of other dogs, you probably want to stay away from parks for good unless you are working with a trainer who supervises your visits. If your dog hasn't been spayed, you may also want to reconsider bringing her to a dog park unless you're interested in raising puppies. Also, if your dog has not been neutered, you should be careful. Of course not all unneutered dogs are aggressive (if yours is, then you shouldn't be there in the first place), but neutered males will often go after an intact male seeking dominance—looking for a fight—and that's no fun for anyone.

Also, although there is nothing cuter than watching puppies play, a dog park is not the place to do it. Puppies are not fully vaccinated until at least four months of age, and diseases they could be exposed to at the dog park, like kennel cough, distemper, and parvo, are dangerous. Moreover, many puppies aren't physically ready to play with big dogs until they reach the six-month mark. They don't have the coordination, physical strength, or socialization to keep them out of harm's way.

My veterinarian urges his clients to use caution regarding taking dogs to dog parks at all. He feels dog parks are definitely off limits for a dog less than six months old, and that owners of older dogs need to make sure the park is well maintained and the "dog park clientele" are healthy and well cared for.

For urbanite owners especially, giving up on the dog park isn't an option; it is the only place your dog can run. So, to keep you and your dog safe, here are some things to look out for and rules to follow.

DOGMA:

Furry Friends

Even if your puppy isn't old enough to go to the dog park, you can and should socialize her. To do this safely, get in touch with friends who have dogs (if you trust that their dogs are healthy) and let their older dog interact with your puppy in a mellow and cootie-free environment. This way, your puppy learns the ropes and stays healthy!

Basics

Before taking your dog to a dog park, you should make sure he has had some basic training. If not, you should consider an obedience class where you can make sure he is friendly to those on both two and four legs, and more importantly, will come when called.

Dog Parking Is Dirty Work

Most dog parks are not maintained by a staff. Instead, it is everyone's responsibility to pitch in and clean up after their dogs. If you leave "presents" behind, it sends a collective message that doing so is acceptable, contributing to a bigger mess. Just remember to bring some hand sanitizer because those poop picker-upper things are revolting!

That said, don't go to the dog park and expect not to get a little dirty. It is a dog park, after all. However, if your dog does dirty someone's clothes, it is polite to apologize and offer to pay the dry-cleaning bill. If you are the "victim," it is similarly polite to respond, "Don't be silly; this is a dog park."

Big Dogs and Little Dogs

They don't always mix well. Many dog parks have areas specifically for smaller dogs, as they often have no idea how small they are and will pick the biggest dogs to play with. This dynamic can be dangerous; instinct sometimes wins over logic, and little dogs can get stuck in the middle.

Irresponsible Dog Owners

There are irresponsible owners at every dog park who don't keep an eye on their dogs or who bring dogs that really shouldn't be there in the first place. Whether it's because the dog is unneutered, has a strong prey drive, or because its play turns violent if provoked, you want to keep your dog as far away as possible. Also, take notice when a dog won't stop humping other dogs. This is not a sexual act, this is assertion of dominance, and it can be a precursor to a fight if the humper picks the wrong humpee.

It's not hard to figure out who these dogs and owners are. Ask around. One thing all dog parks have in common is that everyone likes to talk. People will be more than willing to give you the 411.

Dog Fights

Dog fights often sound a lot worse than they are. However, breaking them up by jumping into the thick of it can escalate the episode and get you injured. While there is no guaranteed way to break up a fight, animal behaviorist Jan Naud recommends Spray Shield Animal Deterrent Spray. It's a citronella-based spray that has proven to be extremely helpful in breaking up dog fights. Water is also a tried-and-true method to break up the intensity of a dog altercation. If neither of these tools are available, it's best to try to break up a fight from the perimeter—taking one of the dogs by the back legs and pulling—almost flinging—them out of the fight while someone else does the same thing with the other dog.

What to Do After a Dog Fight

No matter how good your dog is and how much you try to avoid the unneutered dog that belongs to the creepy guy who smells, fights happen. Unless the attacking dog is a repeat offender or your dog is attacked out of the blue, dog are dogs and playing the blame game is a huge waste of time. Instead, it's most important and productive to focus on assessing your dog's injuries. The involved dogs will most likely be covered in each other's saliva and shaken up, but not always injured. If you see a scratch on the ear or the jowl—two common places for dogs to bite each other—I recommend contacting your vet. If the fight is any more severe than that and there's a puncture wound or an open laceration—especially if there is a size difference between the dogs engaged in the fight—skip the call and go to a vet to get your dog checked out immediately.

Leave the Treats and Special Toys at Home

Some dog parks allow owners to bring in their own toys and treats. This is a recipe for disaster. Fights often start with dogs challenging one another over ownership of a beloved toy or treat. However, if you feel it necessary to bring your dog's favorite toys, only bring in toys that cannot be swallowed by bigger or overeager dogs. And, if you must bring treats for your dog, give them to her away from other dogs. Whatever you do, do not give your treats to other people's dogs without asking permission. Many dogs have allergies or sensitive stomachs and some owners simply prefer they be the only ones allowed to give their dogs treats.

Realities of Dog-Park Dating

Dog parks are a ubiquitous feature in American cities. People love to watch their dogs run, romp, and play. Plus, what's fun for dogs can be equally enjoyable for their owners. Dog parks have become little social scenes. It's like the bar scene, but you don't have to get dressed up and you can go at ten o'clock in the morning on a Sunday in sweats. I admit to having gone on a few dates with a very cute actor whom I met at the Laurel Canyon dog park and I have a friend who met his wife there.

However, while tempting, dating at the dog park can present some potential problems. While the guy with the terrier or the girl with the Bulldog may seem incredibly hot, are you willing to deal with the consequence of seeing said owner after the fact if things don't work out? Just remember, good dog parks are hard to find. Maybe, as with the workplace, a communal house, or a summer share, the adage not to "eat" where you poop should be expanded to include your dog's bathroom habits.

Limits—Learn Your Dog's and Respect Those of Others

Knowing your dog's limits and respecting those of other dogs and their owners are essential to dog-park bliss. The dog park might seem like the ideal environment to exercise any (dog-friendly) pup; however, just as some people don't like parties, some dogs are too overwhelmed by a dog park's crowds and noise to enjoy themselves. So, while you may be enjoying the social aspect of the park, your dog may be miserable. Unfortunately, a scared dog can act out and become aggressive or simply cower in the corner. In either case, it'd be better if you found a more suitable outlet for your dog. Also, even if your dog loves the dog park, remember, dogs do get tired. Be sure to monitor your dog to see if he is cranky and has had enough.

Conversely, when your dog is playing intensely with another dog, it's best to ask the other dog's owner if he is comfortable with the level of play. Similarly, never be afraid to tell another dog's owner that you are uncomfortable with how his dog is interacting with yours.

must love dogs:
dating, day care, and stepping out

A dog needs to be an important aspect of its owner's life. However, having your dog be the only meaningful aspect of your life is a big mistake. Even a tremendously needy dog shouldn't be enough to stop you from having a life, especially a love life. Unless your dog is ill or a very young puppy, you're fooling yourself and committing a major faux pas if you give up human interaction to spend time with your pooch.

As trainer Jan Naud says, "A dog has got to learn to stand on its own at times. Through crate training, and giving a dog chew toys and bones and great things to keep them occupied, you can teach them to be alone. If they don't learn to be alone, then when you have to go to work or out for a date, a dog will sit there and pine. It's miserable for them, and these dogs are the ones that become barkers and end up with psychotic behaviors."

To avoid this common hazard, it's best not to set up unrealistic expectations for your dog. While I'm not suggesting you ignore your dog, especially if you have just gotten her, I encourage you to only coddle her in relation to how you'll care for her in the long run. It's quite common—especially at the beginning of your life with a dog—to let everything else stop and only focus on your pup. This is fine to a certain extent, but if you are spending twenty-four hours a day with your dog, she will get used to that level of attention . . . and any less will send her into a tailspin.

CANINE CONSIDERATION ❖ ❖ ❖

For a happy, healthy dog, indulge her but stay as consistent as possible with your attention.

Dating and Your Dog

One of the biggest challenges of dating when you have a dog is figuring out how they fit into your romantic life. Remember, you can't give up dating to be with your dog . . . even if they seem cuter and more loyal than anyone you've ever dated. Here are some things for the single owner to keep in mind while navigating the dicey world of dating.

What If Your Date Doesn't Like Your Dog, or Vice Versa?

The answer to both questions is quite simple. Even if they seem like an amazing catch, someone who doesn't like your dog may not be right for you. Dogs have an amazing sense about people and often have better radar for potential mates than their owners. Bella loves everyone, but gave one particular guy the cold shoulder when he came to pick me up. It was a setup through friends and he was billed as the nicest guy ever. Somehow, Bella, who loves all people, felt quite differently. She turned her back on him and hid behind me—something very out of character. I made up something to smooth over the awkward moment and we went out on our date. Peter, as I'll call him, was just as he was promoted—a total gentleman—but Bella's bad reaction always stuck in my head. Needless to say, when Peter turned out to be somewhat of a sociopath, I had that "A-ha!" moment when I realized that I should have trusted Bella over my friends who set us up!

It is important to remember that not everyone was raised with dogs or will be comfortable with dogs. If your date admits to not being a fan of dogs, but shows some effort to bond with *your* dog, that's a good sign. However, if they make fun of your dog, belittle your devotion to your dog, or encourage you to forsake your dog—as in, "Can't you just stay over; your dog will be okay"—recognize this as a red flag and move on.

CANINE CONSIDERATION ❖ ❖ ❖

Any date who encourages you to forsake your dog is not respecting you and your responsibilities.

I have burdened/blessed my dear friend Learka by helping her rescue Foxy, a ten-pound Chihuahua/Corgi/Shiba Inu mix who, while a wonderful and loving dog, is also super neurotic and desperately attached. Foxy doesn't take too kindly to Learka giving her attention to another man, and Learka actually calls him "the ultimate cock-block." If Learka is making out on the couch with a guy, Foxy will walk across her shoulders and stop the action. "He will literally put himself between me and the guy and not let us make out." And those are the ones he likes. The ones that he doesn't like don't get off (no pun intended) so easily. Foxy really hated one guy Learka dated and incessantly barked and nipped at him whenever he walked in the house. Foxy does have a bit of a barking and nipping problem, but this time was different; he was unrelenting. Come to find out this guy was a complete nutcase, and Foxy knew it before we did!

While you don't want to exclude a potentially great date, it's best to put your devotion to your dog out there in the beginning of a relationship. If someone balks at this, don't be too sad to cut them loose. Being a single owner will be a far more fulfilling experience than being with someone who doesn't care about the things you care deeply about—namely your dog!

Bedroom Etiquette for the Single Dog Owner

Singletons always want their bedrooms to look as inviting as possible when there's the possibility that a date could turn into a sleepover (or at least a roll in the sheets), but this can be difficult if you own a breed that sheds. Bella sheds like crazy, but she also sleeps with me. So, to make sure my bed looks as inviting as possible at all times—not covered in dog hair—I bought sheets to match her. She's black, so I got a set of black-and-white checked sheets and a black-and-white patterned duvet. This way, no matter what an evening brings, I know my bedding will look as fresh as a daisy.

When you finally get home, there are other issues to consider. Dogs are usually very interested in what their owners are doing, so if you want to get it on with your date but your dog's attention during such intimate moments freaks either of you out, it's advisable to close your bedroom door and let your dog hang out in the living room. One ingenious woman I know recommends that all single owners keep engaging dog treats such as a Kong or a Bully Stick on hand for just such an occasion. Her dog actually gets a little jealous and uncomfortable when she has sex, so she gives him his own treat, shuts her bedroom door, and gets one of her own!

Out and About with Your Canine Companion

One of the best things about having Bella is that I take her almost everywhere with me. In the mornings, we take a walk up Rodeo Drive to get coffee, and our evening walk starts with a stroll through Saks Fifth Avenue—where Bella has become the unofficial therapy dog of the women's shoe department.

Our visits are a treat for everyone. Bella gets showered with kisses, the shoe department is happy, and I get to check out the inventory and dream about actually being able to afford a pair of Louboutins!

People are often surprised that Bella is welcomed with open arms into Saks, Barney's, and other high-end stores in the Beverly Hills area. It's not like she is a purse dog that no one notices; instead, Bella is a big black dog with questionable dog-to-dog skills and a happy tail of utter destruction. So why is she welcomed? The reason is simple: I am a conscientious owner and people trust my dog with me around. You can share the love, too, if you follow a few simple rules of good doggie etiquette.

Pay Attention

When taking your dog into a public place such as a restaurant, store, or to your job (if you're lucky enough), realize that you are no longer only responsible for your own behavior; you are responsible for that of your dog as well. Whatever your dog does, eats, pees on, or knocks over will be a reflection on you, and is your responsibility. For this reason, I am always aware of our surroundings and watch how Bella interacts with people, and especially with other dogs.

CANINE CONSIDERATION ❧ ❧ ❧

Enjoy taking your dog with you, but keep an eye on your dog and what he is doing.

Size Doesn't Matter

Owners of small dogs often assume they don't have to be as conscious as those with big dogs. True, big dogs can intimidate nondog lovers, but little dogs—while less conspicuous and disruptive—can cause big problems. Possibly, because little dogs pose little threat, owners sometimes don't pay attention to what their dogs are doing. This frustrates business owners, as unsupervised dogs can cause problems, including tripping other customers, setting off people's allergies, and of course, the little-dog curse of potty accidents.

Potty Trained

It seems pretty basic, but you'd be surprised at how many people bring dogs who are not potty trained shopping with them. Of course, all dogs have accidents, but remember that a day of shopping or spending the day by your desk—especially for a little dog—can test the bounds of their ability to hold it. It's best to err on the side of caution and give them frequent opportunities to go potty in an appropriate place.

CANINE CONSIDERATION ❖ ❖ ❖

When out and about, give your dog ample chances to go potty. If your dog has an accident, be a considerate dog owner and clean it up.

Don't Be a Rude Dog Owner

When an owner brings their canine companion shopping or to brunch, they should expect people to want to say hello to their dog. Dogs are great stress relievers and really, what brightens a day better than a dog's sweet face? While you don't have to let anyone and everyone pet your dog, it's best to be courteous when people ask. If you have some serious shopping to do or your dog hates crowded places or strangers, leave your dog at home or keep her in her carrier.

To Tie or Not to Tie

Tying your dog up while you run in for a cup of coffee, a quick purchase, or a bite is an unnecessary risk that I strongly encourage owners not to take. While I'm sure the majority of dogs left tied up fare just fine, sadly, some do not. Leaving a dog tied so close to moving cars can have dire consequences if they manage to wiggle out of their collar. The first place they're heading is right into oncoming traffic. Also, unless you're in a small, close-knit community where everyone knows you and your dog, a stranger could easily walk away with your unattended pooch; small dogs especially have been stolen in just this situation. However, if you still feel it necessary to tie your dog up so you can run in to a store or restaurant, please be sure of the following:

1. Your dog is confident being left alone; that he won't have a separation anxiety fit and try to escape and come looking for you; and just as importantly, won't nip or growl at passing strangers
2. Your knot is extremely secure, and your dog is wearing a harness—not a collar that he can slip out of, or a nonslip collar or choke chain with which he can strangle himself
3. Your dog is tied up away from passing cars and out of the way of passersby; while you want your dog to have some area to move around, it's rude to let your dog run amok and get in people's way
4. Check on your dog frequently; make sure he is okay and his leash is securely tied and not twisted—dogs often walk in circles when tied up and their leashes can get so short that they panic

Taking Your Dog to Work

To attract and keep their employees happy and productive, many companies have adopted a pet-friendly workplace policy. In fact, according to a recent *Newsweek* report, 17 percent of American employers allow employees to bring their animal companions to work. If your office has either a well-defined pet policy or one that's a little looser, be sure you and your dog can take full advantage of the privilege by taking the following into consideration:

1. Only bring dogs to the office if they should be there and want to be there. Dogs who aren't well socialized, potty trained, clean, vaccinated, or able to be left alone in your office without having a meltdown should be left at home. And remember, if your dog doesn't thrive in social situations, don't force it. She is still a great dog, she's just happier in her own space. Pushing her into a work environment could lead to bigger problems than having to pay for a midday dog walker.

2. Be considerate of others. Keep your dog in your own workspace. Hallways and common areas should not become de facto dog parks. It's not fair to those who seek a more peaceful work environment and it increases the possibility of a dog park–style dogfight.

3. Take frequent, but not excessive potty breaks. It's important to avoid potty accidents inside the office, but don't take advantage and use your dog as an excuse to take breaks—you'll set yourself up for coworker resentment.

4. Dog-proof your space. Make your dog's integration into your office a smooth one by making your workspace pet friendly. Keep office equipment such as computers safe from a potential puppy pull-down by keeping wires tucked away out of reach. Bring in a comfy bed for your dog and provide chew toys to keep her busy.

5. Stay Spot. Provide your dog an accessible yet out-of-the-way spot where she can safely and comfortably chill, whether you're in the office or not. Bringing a crate or installing a baby gate can create such a space. And, if you're going to be out of the office for an extended period of time, ask someone to

check in on your pooch to make sure she is doing okay without you.

Leaving Your Dog in the Car

Pretty much every owner has left their dog in the car at some point for some amount of time. Some dogs love the car, but others loathe it and panic taking one step toward your vehicle. If your dog hates the car, please don't consider leaving them—not even for five minutes while you run into Starbucks for a latte. But if your dog fares okay in the car and it's legal to leave him unattended, here are some tips to keep him as safe as possible.

1. Lock your windows in a semi-raised position so your dog has an ample airflow, but can't escape through the window if he panics. This gets a bit tricky if you have hand-crank windows. Check your car's manual to see if there is a way to lock your windows.

2. Set your parking brake. A panicky pup running around inside your car can take your car out of gear and send it rolling.

3. Never leave your dog in your car if it's over 72°F outside or 70°F if the car is in direct sunlight. The temperature inside a car can spike twenty to thirty degrees above the outside temperature, a sad fact that kills hundreds of dogs each year and gets many people in big trouble. I saw an angry mob descend upon one woman who had irresponsibly left two dogs in her Volvo sedan while shopping. The dogs were panting and scared, and she was rightfully read the riot act.

4. Protect your dog from cold weather with blankets, a sweater, or even a heating pad. Bigger dogs with thick coats and a healthy layer of body fat should be fine down to about 30°F. However, smaller dogs and older dogs have little of either

to protect them from the elements; leaving them in a freezing or near-freezing car could be seriously damaging to their health.

5. Turn off your car alarm. A dog moving around inside your car will most likely set it off and the noise, which is bad for us, is devastating for them. However, without the protection of your alarm, it is possible for your dog—especially if he is little—to be stolen. To keep him safe but avoid the alarm being set off, keep all doors locked and the windows open just enough to let a breeze flow through the car or, better yet, if your dog is small enough, take him with you.

6. Remove your dog's leash before leaving him in the car alone. It can get caught, twist, and end up strangling your dog.

Day Care and Boarding

One of the key challenges for a single owner is balancing your single life with taking excellent care of your dog. Regrettably, these two things are not always compatible. Single owners have jobs, are in school, have dates, and go out of town. However, even the most independent and potty-trained dogs can't care for themselves. Dogs left alone too long without supervision can get destructive and destructive behavior is one of the top reasons dogs are given up by their owners. So, if you're going to be out of town or away for the night, you're going to have to make some arrangements for your dog's care. Figuring out what those plans are going to be plus contemplating the idea of leaving your dog with someone else can be overwhelming. And truly, it should be. Deciding who watches your dog is not a decision to be made without careful consideration. You can't trust just anyone or any facility with your dog's care. Dog walkers, doggie day care, kennels, friends—there are many options, and not all dogs will thrive within each environment.

I'm embarrassed to admit it, but Bella got kicked out of day care in Seattle and demoted from cage-free boarding to a kennel run at a facility here in L.A. when she jumped the front counter to come looking for me after I dropped her off. Thankfully, with time and training Bella's tolerance for boarding has increased and her anxiety about me leaving wears off more quickly. But, because of her anxiety and her strength, I remain extremely conservative about where she stays and who watches her when I can't.

If your dog is a generally easy dog, which admittedly Bella is not, your choices will be far greater than if your dog has separation anxiety or other behavioral problems. Here's a breakdown of your options and a few things to look out for in each case.

DOGMA:

Show You Care

When you're going to be gone for an extended period of time, let your dog know you're thinking of him by sending a doggie care package! When my friend Daphne goes out of town, she leaves her Labrador, Idaho, with a trusted dog sitter, but also sends special care packages complete with chew toys, tennis balls (Idaho's favorite), and a recently worn T-shirt that still smells like her.

Dog Sitters/Dog Walkers

Dog walking and sitting services are available in most cities and towns across the country. While specifics vary, the general concept is that someone will come to your house to walk and spend time with your dog for a set period of time—usually fifteen minutes, thirty minutes, or an hour at a time—for a fee. Dog-walking services usually offer overnight care as well, with a pet sitter staying in your home with your pup while you travel.

▼ Choosing a Dog Sitter/Dog Walker

As with any service, getting a referral for a dog walker is essential; you'll be giving these people access to your home and entrusting them with your dog, which is not something to be taken lightly. A dog walker doesn't have to be a rocket scientist, but realize that they're the ones who will be making sure your dog doesn't get hit by a car, get in a fight at the park, or escape through an unlocked gate. If a walker isn't familiar with dogs, he may not be able to anticipate problems that could seriously injure your pooch. Be sure to ask questions, especially in regards to your walker's personal experience and knowledge of canine behavior. Also, in addition to checking references, check his license and bonding information. If he doesn't have a license or isn't bonded, you don't want him.

▼ Things to Look Out For

Dog sitting and walking is a great business for dog-loving entrepreneurs to get into. That can be good for you; my dog walker is a brilliant, well-educated, articulate actress who is extremely trustworthy. The flexibility of the hours allows her to pursue her career. On the flip side, pretty much anyone can get business cards printed and deem themselves a dog walker. If using a smaller service, you have to be that much more vigilant about checking references.

Larger pet walking/sitting services present challenges, as well. The larger operations employ numerous underling walkers and have been known to switch walkers without informing you. Hopefully, whatever service you use has thoroughly checked all employees, but that isn't always the case. Plus, while you may be paying $20 for a fifteen-minute walk, a dog walker working for a service is only making $9 or $10 for the entire hour. This is not a job that always draws top-notch people, so, if you're using a larger service, be sure to check out whoever is coming to your house and stipulate that no one can walk your dog unless you have met them first.

CANINE CONSIDERATION ❖ ❖ ❖

If you're using a smaller dog-walking service, checking references is of the utmost importance. If you're using a larger service with multiple dog walkers, be sure you know who is walking your dog and gaining access to your home.

Doggie Day Care

Within the last few years, doggie day cares, especially the cage-free variety, have become extremely popular. Most frequently, doggie day cares are large spaces with ample room for dogs to run and play. A certain number of staff members will be in the mix with the dogs to break up any altercations and generally keep an eye out.

▼ Choosing a Doggie Day Care

Not all doggie day cares are created equal, and expense doesn't always mean quality or appropriateness for your dog.

When choosing a doggie day care, always seek referrals and visit any facility you're considering in person. What is your gut reaction? Is it clean? Is it crowded? How are the dogs handled? What is the staff like? Are they certified in pet first aid? If anything makes you uneasy, it's best to look for another facility.

Once you have found a place that fits your criteria, think about your dog. Is she well suited for this particular day care? Some are fast-paced, frenetic environments with tons of stimulation and others offer a more consistently mellow, quiet environment. You know your dog best, and can choose accordingly. Also, some larger facilities will have numerous play areas going at one time— one for bigger, more energetic dogs, one for small dogs, and still another for older dogs. Be sure your dog gets into the right room!

▼ Things to Look Out For

When shopping for a cage-free facility, it's important to closely evaluate the staff and management. To keep up with demand, doggie day cares have sprouted up all over the country. While it's harder to open your own day care facility than it is to open a dog-walking operation, there are many novices entering the day-care business. The owner doesn't have to be a dog expert, but it is essential that there is a trainer or manager on staff and on the premises who has years of experience handling dogs. As opposed to a kennel where dogs don't often interact with one another in situations where one can get hurt, cage-free kenneling can be one big fight waiting to happen. Lack of experience can be dangerous in this environment.

Also, if you wish to use a doggie day care for boarding, it is important to find out how a facility handles their overnight care. Are dogs crated? Do they sleep in a particular area? Before boarding overnight, ask to see these areas and decide if you feel comfortable with the arrangements. Most importantly, ask if someone sleeps in the facility overnight. Dogs are often left alone overnight at day cares and boarding facilities without supervision. That just doesn't work for me; I never leave Bella unattended at night, so why should they?

CANINE CONSIDERATION ❖ ❖ ❖

Scrutinize any doggie day care or cage-free boarding facility, and be sure to interview staff and management regarding their policies and experience with dogs.

Kennel

While doggie day cares have only recently gained in popularity, kennels have been around for decades. Standard kennels tend to be more rigid environments than their cage-free counterparts. At most kennels, dogs stay in dog runs—fenced areas where your pup can run back and forth. At other kennels, dogs stay in crates for the majority of the day. In either case, dogs should be brought out to get exercise and do their business either on a leash or in a yard.

▼ Choosing a Kennel

Kennels can get a bad rap, sometimes deservedly so. Leaving a dog in a cold run or confined to a crate isn't the ideal choice for indulgent owners. However, if you have a challenging dog who doesn't thrive in cage-free situations—Hello, Bella—or you're cost conscious, kennels tend to be more affordable than cage-free day care facilities. The good news is that you can find good kenneling options.

Be sure any kennel you choose provides your dog with as comfortable an environment as possible. Do the runs provide ample protection from the elements? Is there good air circulation? Does the place smell clean? As with cage-free boarding, you must take a tour of any facility you're considering. The pictures they show on their website may not always match up to the reality.

▼ **Things to Look Out For**

Unlike cage-free options, kennels have only a set number of spaces. At holiday time, kennels will sometimes overbook and instead of turning people away, will board some dogs in crates. While not necessarily a crime, having your dog stay in a crate versus a run, especially for big dogs, may not be acceptable.

DOGMA:

Pack a Lunch

Always bring your dog's own food with you when dropping him off at a kennel. While the facility may offer food as part of their services, chances are it won't be the same food your dog is currently eating, and the change could cause stomach upset.

CANINE CONSIDERATION ❖ ❖ ❖

Kenneling your dog may be unavoidable for cost reasons or because your dog doesn't thrive in a cage-free environment. So, find the best kennel you can by visiting and making sure it's up to your standards.

Friends

Hopefully, you have a friend that you can trust to watch your dog when you go out of town or can't make it home after work. While this may seem like the best option, there are a few things to think about before you go this route.

▼ Choosing a Friend

While many of your friends may love your dog, they won't all be willing or able to handle the responsibility of caring for even the best-behaved pooch. Be exceptionally careful about which friend you choose to bestow this responsibility/opportunity on, as it may be a huge transition for someone who is unused to the commitment of dog ownership. It may be best to choose someone who has a dog themselves or has had a dog in the past and won't feel overwhelmed by the responsibility. You don't want to ruin a friendship with a bad dog-sitting experience.

▼ Things to Look Out For

If you have an easygoing dog, leaving him in the care of a responsible friend should be fine. However, if your dog has any issues such as separation anxiety or aggression, you may be putting your dog and your friendship in jeopardy.

Recently I found myself helping Lucian, a very talented composer and single friend, search the greater Los Angeles area for Gumbo; his sweet as sugar but painfully shy Boxer mix who tunneled out of his well-fenced yard in the middle of the night while a friend dog sat. Even though the friend was trustworthy and careful, Gumbo's separation anxiety paired with his skills as an escape artist prevailed. When Lucian's friend woke up, Gumbo was gone.

For more than two months Lucian agonized over Gumbo's whereabouts. He checked and rechecked shelters, posted fliers, and scoured the Internet for leads. His whole life became trying to find Gumbo. And while there were numerous possible sightings of Gumbo-like dogs all over the city, nothing panned out until a full nine weeks later.

A woman who had seen one of the numerous posters of Gumbo, spotted a similar-looking dog playing in a backyard about two miles from Lucian's house. Figuring it was a long shot, the Good Samaritan stopped to take a closer look. Thankfully, it was Gumbo. He had been hanging around the neighborhood for a couple of weeks, playing with one particular family's dog during the day and sleeping in their garden at night. He refused to let anyone close enough to read his tag, but happily ate all the meals the family prepared for him.

Those two months were horrendous but thankfully Gumbo's story had a happy ending. Unfortunately, most don't and, while no one is squarely to blame in such situations, asking a friend to care for a needy or challenging dog is a mistake. When you ask a friend to stay with your dog or your dog to stay with them, they are doing you a favor for free. In life, you often get what you pay for.

Acknowledging that Bella has a few issues, I always factor boarding costs into any trip budget. I know I won't enjoy myself if I'm worried about her. I have also found a great dog sitter and a fantastic kennel. In both situations, I know Bella will be well cared for and I know I can call at any hour of the day to check in.

Knowing that someone is being paid to care for Bella makes me feel more comfortable than if a friend were doing it as a favor, but that's me. Many owners have great success with friends watching their dog. The truth is you just have to be careful and honest with yourself. Is your dog okay to be left in the care of someone not being paid to watch him? And is your friend up to that responsibility?

CANINE CONSIDERATION ❖ ❖ ❖

If you're going to trust someone to watch your dog, make sure your dog and your friend are up to the task.

Before You Use Any of These Options

You must be honest with yourself about your dog's needs and with whoever will be watching her. If your dog is aggressive, hates female dogs, or tends to try to escape after you drop her off, you must disclose this information. While these truths may be embarrassing, they will allow the people watching your dog to take the best possible care of her.

Or, if the idea of boarding your dog while you travel just doesn't appeal, you can always consider bringing her along.

nine

on a wing and a paw: your traveling pooch

As American society embraces pets as integral parts of our lives, it has become easier and easier to travel with your four-legged friend. Instead of having to sneak a pooch into your hotel room, hospitality chains ranging from Motel 6 (which offers more than 800 dog-friendly motels across the country) to Four Seasons Hotels are eager to welcome you and your pup as their guests. Kimpton Hotels (*www.kimptonhotels.com*) even offers amazing "Pet Packages" ranging from the basics—beds, food bowls, wee-wee pads, and poop bags—to the decadent—psychic readings for your dog.

Finding a hotel as welcoming as a Kimpton is a treat, but being prepared goes beyond finding pet-friendly lodging. Just as all Kimpton hotels offer important information on nearby pet-friendly parks, dog-friendly restaurants, dog sitting, and walking and grooming services, as a responsible owner, you must make similar preparations of your own. Websites such as *www.dogfriendly.com* and the magic of a Google search can make preparatory research far easier, but don't wait until you get to a location to do your homework. Whether you're staying at a friend's house or a five-star hotel, being prepared can mean the difference between a successful trip and disaster. Be sure you have the following items prepared to get yourself and your dog ready to go, no matter your destination:

- Food
- Water
- Bowls
- Treats (chew toys)
- Medications
- Picture of your dog (in case you, God forbid, have to make a lost sign)
- ID tag with your cell phone or local information
- Leashes
- Extra towel
- Bed
- Vaccination record/Health certificate
- List of local resources—vets, parks, doggie day cares

Now that you have your supplies ready, there is the small matter of getting to your destination with a happy, healthy pooch and your sanity intact. Traveling with a dog—whether by car or air—can be quite stressful. Here are some helpful tips on getting there—wherever *there* is—with as little stress as possible.

Traveling By Car

Many owners opt to travel by car instead of by air, especially those who have larger dogs who would have to travel as cargo. Taking a road trip with your pooch can be awesome (I drove with Bella from Los Angeles to Seattle and it was an amazing experience). Here are a few things I have learned from my experience and from those of other road-tripping owners.

Bella loves to ride in the car and, as I had found her while driving in downtown Los Angeles, she thinks of my car as her safe place. But not all dogs feel this way about cars. For many dogs, the only time they get in the car is to go to the vet or the groomer, not great associations. So, if you are planning a road trip with a pooch that gets stressed about car rides, help her make a new car connection. Make her associate the car with something positive. Take her by car to a new dog park or across town for a walk in a new neighborhood. Even letting your dog sit in your car to eat a treat and then get out will help her reassign the meaning of the car from negative to positive. One ingenious owner I know brought his dog to an old drive-in theater every day for a week before taking her on a long road trip. He watched a movie and she got over her fear of the car.

For some dogs, no amount of desensitization will make them overcome travel anxiety. If this is the case, don't panic. Talk to your vet about medications such as Xanax or Lorazepan, which will undercut your dog's anxiety and make for a smoother time on the road. If you're against doping up your dog, try a homeopathic option such as lavender, valerian, or Rescue Remedy.

The Vomit Quotient

With some dogs, there is the additional fun issue of motion sickness. And nothing gets a road trip off to a bad start like a car that has been blessed with doggie vomit. You will, of course, have extra towels on hand, but if you know your dog is prone to motion sickness, it's best to cut the vomit issue off at the pass by restricting food before your drive or giving your pooch an antinausea/motion sickness drug such as Benadryl (consult your vet for dosage). This is something I learned the hard way when traveling with my friend Susan and her beagle, Snoopy.

Susan was at the point where she wanted to get a second dog, so we made a plan to visit a German Shepherd rescue facility just outside L.A. Knowing that it was essential for any dog Susan got to get along with her beagle, Snoopy, we planned to bring him with us. Since she had a two-seater convertible and I had a wagon, I agreed to drive. There was only one problem: Snoopy was prone

DOGMA:

Holistic Healing

Many vets are unfamiliar with alternative-medicine approaches. If your vet thinks it's hocus pocus, but you'd like to explore an alternative approach, you might be going to the wrong vet. Visit the American Holistic Veterinary Medical Association at *www.ahvma.org* to find an alternative vet in your area.

to car sickness. To avoid an accident, Susan opted to wait until we got back from our outing to feed Snoopy. Unfortunately, Snoopy had a different plan.

When Snoopy realized he would not be given a morning meal, he took it upon himself to find one on his own. He managed to find and open an Igloo cooler belonging to one of the painters working on Susan's house. Snoopy helped himself to a burrito filled with all sorts of goodies that he later shared with us on a very upsetting ride on the freeway as he moaned, groaned, and threw up burrito all over the back of my poor car. Thankfully, we had numerous towels, all of which were promptly thrown out upon arrival at the German Shepherd rescue.

Although my car needed a bath in Nature's Miracle after our trip, it was well worth it. That day Susan adopted a handsome, 120-pound German Shepherd named Duke, and I learned that burritos, beagles, and backseats don't mix!

CANINE CONSIDERATION ❖ ❖ ❖

Be sure not to feed your dog for at least a few hours before taking off on a road trip of any length—and always bring plenty of towels!

Traveling by Plane

Sometimes traveling by car simply isn't an option, and you'll have to fly with your pooch. Although we've all heard horror stories about dogs on planes getting lost or worse, most dogs do get there in one piece and not much worse for wear. That said, flying with your dog can be intimidating and anxiety provoking. Here's the lowdown on what to expect and what you can do to be prepared.

Under the Seat

A deciding factor when flying with your dog is whether she is small enough to travel with you as a carry-on or if she must go in the belly of the plane as cargo. Flying with your dog under the seat versus under the plane is quite a different process and, if your dog is almost small enough to fit under the seat, I would never tell you to fudge it, but . . . traveling with a dog this way is a far more pleasant experience. For better or worse, though, you can't go by weight alone to assess whether your pet qualifies for under the seat. Instead, as a general rule of thumb, your dog has to be able to turn around in a carrier that is airline approved. So, to give you every possible inch and chance to make it on the plane with your dog, I recommend getting an official Sherpa Brand bag (*www.sherpapet.com*). According to their website, "The Sherpa Bag is now the officially approved soft-sided carrier for in-cabin use on the following airlines: Air Canada, Alaska, American, America West, Continental, Delta, Northwest, TWA, United and US Airways."

DOGMA:

Clean Scene

Nature's Miracle is God's gift to dog owners. It magically removes the odor and stain residue of most doggie accidents.

Having that official Sherpa seal of approval removes any question as to whether or not your carrier will be accepted from airline to airline. And the fact that it is soft sided will give your dog some wiggle room and help the carrier fit more easily under an airline seat.

So, if you're lucky enough to have a dog that passes the under-the-seat test, flying is relatively easy. Here is what you need to do.

▼ Book Your Pet a Ticket in Advance

Each airline has its own in-flight pet policies. On American Airlines, "pets traveling in the cabin require a reservation to ensure no more than seven pets are booked on any single flight." Continental Airlines prohibits dogs under the seat on flights to and from Hawaii, but it does allow four dogs in the main cabin on all Continental and Continental Micronesia and Continental Express flights. It's pretty hard to keep track of all the various airlines' rules, but one thing is certain for all of them—you better book a ticket for your dog.

▼ At the Airport

With travel today, most airlines want you to check in at least an hour or more before the flight. If you're flying across the country, this means your dog may not get a chance to go potty for seven or more hours. If you can, check in with your dog then walk around the airport to find a nice potty place for him. Try to hang around outside as long as possible. Once inside the terminal, depending on the airport, your freedom to let your dog roam could be limited. It's a good idea to give your dog a hearty walk either at home before you leave or at the airport. Having your dog a bit pooped from exercise will keep him calm on the flight.

▼ Screening Your Dog

Per Transportation Security Administration (TSA) policy, all owners must present their dog to security officers at the carry-on screening checkpoint. You may then walk your dog through the metal detector with you. If this is not possible, your dog will have to undergo a secondary screening, including a visual and physical inspection by security officers.

Your dog should never be placed through an X-ray machine. If a TSA screener tries to make you do that, say no (nicely) and ask for a supervisor. However, you may be asked to remove your dog from her carrier so the carrier can be X-rayed.

▼ Health Certificate

Most airlines require health certificates for all dogs traveling. Health certificates must be issued by a licensed vet ten days or less prior to flying. A health certificate verifies that a dog has his shots, is in good health, and able to fly.

▼ Get Your Dog Used to Being in Her Carrier

Once you get your dog's ticket and health certificate in order, you must get her accustomed or reaccustomed to whatever bag or crate she will be traveling in. Whether your dog is perfectly crate trained or was the last time you traveled, for your own sanity, be sure in advance of your trip that she is cool with her traveling accommodations. If she hates her bag or crate and makes a fuss about being in it, you will not be popular on your flight. So, in the days leading up to your trip, take your crate or Sherpa bag out of the closet and set it out for your dog to inspect and get accustomed to. Just like you did when you were crate training, put some treats in it and get her excited about the prospect of spending time in her "traveling home."

DOGMA:

Airline Etiquette

It's a little mind-numbing to keep track of which airline has which rules, as they are ever changing. A great site to use for domestic travel with your pet is *www.petflight.com* and for international travel check out *www.pettravel.com*. These comprehensive sites allow you to research the travel policies of many major airlines and many countries.

Wishing to skip the $50–$100 fee for bringing a dog onboard, some owners I know fly with their dogs without buying a proper ticket. Many dog carriers look a lot like regular carry-on bags, so they simply walk on-board without a second look. Although it's tempting to save the money, this is a bad idea. Airlines can terminate your travel for pretty much any reason these days. If you are caught sneaking your dog on a flight, you might get away with simply paying the fee you would have had to pay anyway or if they are at pet capacity or being difficult you could be kicked off your flight entirely. This isn't worth it, especially if you're caught between connecting flights. You and your dog could end up stuck at an airport with no flight and no place to stay.

Buy a Sherpa bag, always have your dog's ticket and health certificate on hand, and make sure your dog has had ample opportunity to potty before getting on the plane. Talk to your veterinarian about tranquilizers, but don't be surprised if he advises against them.

Under the Plane (Big Dogs)

For owners of larger breeds who must travel as cargo in the belly of the plane, there is more preparation, anxiety, and unfortunately, risk. Many traveling pet owners simply choose to keep their four-legged friends either in the care of a trusted friend, a dog sitter, or a kennel instead of taking them on the trip. There is no right or wrong answer. For some, traveling with their larger dog is a way of life while others couldn't bear to place their dog under the plane. Only you can make that decision. But if you make the decision to fly with your dog, here's how to do it right.

▼ Choosing Your Flight

Every airline has its own unique rules regarding pets traveling as baggage. While all airlines must comply with federal rules regarding handling dogs—keeping dogs out of direct sunlight and maintaining normal cabin pressure in the baggage compartment when animals are present—accidents do happen. To review timely information on different airlines' policies as well as recent records of incidents involving pets traveling as baggage, go to *www.petflight.com*.

If the details of traveling with your dog as baggage seem like too much to deal with, there are pet concierge services to help you maneuver the process of getting your pup from Point A to Point B. Services such as *www.pacpet.com* have relationships with airlines and know the tricks of the trade to assure your pet has as good a trip as possible. But, if the additional cost of a concierge is prohibitive, you can be your dog's personal travel agent, making sure that even if he has to travel in the belly of the plane his best interests are served.

▼ Connecting Flights

When traveling with your dog as baggage, always, always, always choose the most direct flights possible. Connections can be rough on dogs traveling as cargo. By adding a stop, you increase the chance of your dog being lost.

Sometimes connections are unavoidable. If this is the case, be ready to do some running through the airport and perhaps be a bit pushy. To avoid having your dog misplaced during a connection, it is up to you to make sure your dog actually gets from plane A to plane B. To accomplish this, book a seat as far forward as possible so that you can get off the plane ASAP. You want to be able to watch the luggage being unloaded from the plane, and your best vantage point will mostly likely be from inside the terminal. If you don't see your dog's crate, go to a gate agent immediately to have them check on your dog. Don't back down; you are your dog's only advocate here. If you do not see your dog or get confirmation of your dog's whereabouts, do everything you can to make sure that plane doesn't take off again.

Once at the connecting flight—you may have to run like a crazy person here—make sure your dog is loaded onto the plane. Again, don't let that flight take off until you have confirmation that your dog is safely on-board. Ask the flight attendant whether the flight will be grounded at your destination or be continuing on to another stop. If this is the last stop, try to relax. There is little risk of your dog being misrouted at this point. However, if the flight is continuing on to another city, again, sit in the front and make sure your dog gets off the plane. If you don't see your crate being unloaded, go straight to the gate agent to have them check on your dog's whereabouts.

Fortunately, even with connections, the vast majority of dogs do make it to their destinations without incident. So once you see your dog's crate come off, go down to the baggage claim and breathe a sigh of relief!

▼ Reserve Your Dog's Spot

Once you've researched flights, it is important to contact whichever airline you think works best for your itinerary and check to make sure there is availability for your dog to travel as baggage. Many airlines limit the number of animals they will accept for each flight. You don't want to end up booking a ticket only to find out there is no room for your dog.

▼ Maybe Meds, Maybe Not

If you're anything like me, you may need a sedative to calm yourself down when sending your dog as baggage—but your dog may not. Many vets recommend against sedating dogs traveling as cargo. The effects of tranquilizers at higher altitudes can be unpredictable, even dangerous, and you won't be there to keep an eye on her. It is a difficult call; discuss it with your vet. Every dog is different and your vet may feel your dog needs to be sedated. Do whatever your vet says and follow her dosage advice.

▼ Let Your Crate Do the Talking

At some point, no matter how nervous you are, you're going to have to put your dog in the hands of the airline. A good way to stay there as much as you can without literally crawling in with him is to decorate your crate. I'm not talking about making it cute; I mean make that crate stand out so it can be more easily seen and give your dog a voice: "HI, MY NAME IS BELLA AND I'M GOING TO 124 MAIN STREET, LA, CA 90024"; "I am very sweet"; "Thank you for taking care of me on my flight." Don't be afraid to make it really stand out! Border Collie Rescue recommends putting reflective tape on your dog's crate so it can be seen easily even on a foggy night or in the dark. I also recommend taping a recent photo of your pup to the crate in case your dog somehow escapes his kennel. Likewise, put a copy of your dog's health certificate and any other important contact information in a plastic bag and attach it to the back of the crate in case of an emergency. Don't be shy—the more information the better!

International Travel

For you international jetsetters traveling with pooches in tow, all of the above rules still apply. But, as you might expect, the duration of international flights as well as customs regulations and quarantines regarding animals coming into and out of foreign countries add a few more steps to the process. Be sure to educate yourself about these additional steps by checking with the counsel general for the country you plan to visit. Print out a copy of that country's policies and procedures for incoming pets so that you may share it with your vet. That way he can provide you with the complete health certificate you need to get your pet safely accepted at your destination.

To help protect your dog and avoid problems, take the following steps:

- Confirm your dog's reservation
- Fly direct if possible
- If forced to book a connecting flight, be your dog's advocate during transfer
- Fly in the morning
- Watch the weather
- Be sure your dog is wearing an ID with valid phone number
- Provide food and water
- ID your dog's crate and make it as noticeable as possible

ten

dealing with the hard stuff

On the flipside of all the fun times you'll have with your dog, there will also be the inevitable hard times. While living through a dog's decline or losing a dog isn't ever going to be easy, here is some sound advice for making it through.

Saying Goodbye

In writing this book, I have witnessed firsthand the deep bond between single dog owners and their beloved four-legged friends.

"I love Tallulah so much; I'm scared that when I have kids I won't even love them as much."

"I can't tell you how much pride I feel that I could walk across the United States, and Amber wouldn't leave my side once. She would defiantly chase a cat or two, but the sound of my voice would bring her bounding in my direction like a miniature, furry Tyrannosaurus rex—all teeth and happiness."

"I can't go anywhere and not feel like I miss Dolly. I can't do anything, even be at work, and not think 'Is she okay?'"

It is for these reasons that I have included this sad but extremely necessary section on helping an owner get through a very dark day—the day you have to say goodbye to your beloved canine companion. In dog circles, the death of a dog is often referred to as a dog crossing the Rainbow Bridge. While it may sound cheesy, the term comes from a well-known poem by an unknown author who believes that when a dog is old or is suffering, it is best to let them move on to another, happier place. I'm not suggesting that you unnecessarily or prematurely put your dog to sleep or give up when there is hope or if cost is the only thing standing between you and your dog's health. What I am saying is not to fall into the all-too-common trap of holding onto your dog longer than you should because you can't bear to say goodbye. Giving a dog relief from illness or age is the most loving and humane thing an owner can do.

Your dog has been selfless in her love for you, and now it's your turn. Allowing self-interest to dictate your dog's last days will be something you'll regret. Remember: It's not the quantity but the quality of the time you and your dog have together that matters most.

CANINE CONSIDERATION ❖ ❖ ❖

Always consider what's in your dog's best interest when making decisions regarding saying goodbye.

Deciding When to Say Goodbye

Deciding on the right time to let a dog go is not only heartbreaking, it can be confusing as well. There is no definitive point at which you can say, "Oh yes, we've crossed this line so it's definitely time." It should be that easy, but it's not. Dogs need to move on from this life for all sorts of reasons: disease, injury, infirmity, old age. Also, even though I am an avid rescuer and loathe the idea—there are some dogs that, due to their anxiety and aggression, are better off moving over the Rainbow Bridge in a loving way rather than being sent to a shelter and euthanized. Whatever the situation, it is up to you alone to make the call when the time comes.

My vet's very sage advice regarding this difficult decision is to think how far you would want to walk in your dog's shoes. If you say, "I wouldn't want to live in that condition"—whether that condition is pain, uncontrollable anxiety, or weakness—then you shouldn't be putting your dog through it, either.

If you still can't let go, seek the counsel of someone you trust who has been in this situation. While you can't live your life by committee decision, it is helpful to get other people's perspectives to help generate your own. Your vet and her staff should be a good resource for this. You can't ask them to make the decision for you, but you can and should ask what they would do if this were their own dog. Also, check out the Internet, where you can find numerous message boards, blogs, and social networking sites dedicated to pet health care. While you should check with your vet about any medical advice you find online, the camaraderie and support can help get you through a tough time.

CANINE CONSIDERATION ❖ ❖ ❖

Ask your vet or a trusted veterinary tech what they would do if it were their dog. They will be familiar with the medical realities, and personalizing the question will bring thoughtful guidance.

Making It as Easy as Possible on Yourself and Your Dog

Once you have made the decision to put your dog to sleep, there are still a few choices to be made. Here are a few tips that might make the process a little easier.

▼ To Be There or Not to Be There

Deciding whether or not you want to be in the room when your dog is given the injection is something you must decide for yourself. It might just be too much for some to handle, and it is very common for people to say their goodbyes while their dog is still alive and then let the doctor administer the injection. Sometimes people will then want to go back in to say a final goodbye. I can't tell you what is right and what is wrong; but I can tell you that while it's incredibly sad, there is a certain peace in knowing that you were with your dog until the end. I'm sad to report that I have been through the euthanasia process with many dogs (some from rescue, some with friends, and some family dogs). In each case, without fail, I have been glad that I was there with the dog as he or she passed on. Plus, in each case I found myself surprised by how peaceful a process it can be.

▼ Making the Appointment

Once you've decided it's time to let your dog go, be sure to make an appointment with your vet at a time when the office is as quiet as possible. Also, be sure the person taking your appointment knows why you're coming in. That way they can schedule the rest of their appointments accordingly.

▼ Make Your Dog as Comfortable as Possible

If your dog really hates going to the vet, ask your vet for a sedative in advance. There is no need to make a dog's final moments any more stressful than they need to be. To this same end, you may want to consider one of the new at-home euthanasia services around the country. To find a reputable service in your area, ask your vet. If they don't have one, contact your groomer, a local rescue, or breed club for a referral.

▼ Ask Questions

In the days and weeks leading up to having to put your dog down, you will most likely be going to your vet on a more regular basis, unless your dog's crossing is the result of an accident. At these appointments, it's a good idea to ask your vet what the procedure will be like. Different vets use different protocols and it is best that you are prepared for the process.

▼ Everyone Deals Differently

Remember, there is no right or wrong way to act when it's time to say goodbye to your dog. Everyone grieves and deals with situations differently, so don't judge yourself for any sort of weird freak-out you may have. Grieving for your dog as someone else might grieve the loss of a person is normal; don't let anyone criticize the way you react. It is common for an owner to get extremely depressed after the loss of their pet. If you find yourself really losing it, support is available through websites such as *www.petloss. com* and the pet-loss support hotline operated by the University of California at Davis Veterinary School. Staffed by veterinary students trained by a professional grief counselor, this hotline "provides a non-judgmental outlet for people to express their feelings and concerns when faced with difficult times involving their cherished animal companions."

CANINE CONSIDERATION ❖ ❖ ❖

Allow yourself to grieve for the loss of your pet, and ask for help from friends and professionals if necessary.

Cost Factor

One of the many sad factors to consider when deciding whether or not to put your dog down is the cost of keeping him alive. It's tragic to think that if you had all the money in the world you might be able to keep a dog alive, but can't because you're a single person who sometimes struggles to make rent.

We can't always budget for big vet bills, and many dogs are put down because the cost to keep them alive exceeds the owner's means. There is even a name for this phenomenon: economic euthanasia. While I would sell my left kidney to keep Bella alive, you don't often have time to get things in order when a dog gets sick. It is for this reason that I encourage all owners to get pet insurance. However, if you didn't get pet insurance or can't meet the deductible at crisis time, there are some amazing resources out there to help you.

▼ Never Underestimate the Charity of Others

There are 501(c3) charities such as *www.thepetfund.com* and *www.angels4animals.org* dedicated to helping pet owners who could not otherwise afford to keep their pets healthy and alive. From Angels 4 Animals:

"Thousands of pets are put to sleep by reluctant pet owners, who are faced with financial challenges that prohibit them from rendering emergency and necessary medical care for their animals. . . . Angels4Animals has a mission to serve as the guardian angel of animals whose caretakers find themselves in difficult financial situations. At Angels4Animals we believe that animal owners should not have to say goodbye to the animals that they love."

How awesome is that? For more groups, go to *www.cavycare inc.org/help_w_vet_bills.htm*. This site, provided by, of all places, a guinea-pig sanctuary, offers a comprehensive list of wonderful groups willing to help in not-so-wonderful situations.

DOGMA:

Don't Go It Alone

Try to avoid putting your dog down alone if at all possible. Bring a friend, even if they wait in the car for you; being by yourself and having to drive home in an emotionally traumatized state could be dangerous.

dealing with the hard stuff

Less formal than this route, many pet owners have turned to *www.craigslist.org* and their Myspace or Facebook groups to help raise funds to save their dogs. While this may not be comfortable for everyone, there is money to be raised. People you don't even know might connect to your story and could conceivably call your vet with hundreds of dollars in donations.

CANINE CONSIDERATION ❖ ❖ ❖

It's best to save in case of an emergency, but if you need help to save your dog's life, don't be afraid to ask for it.

▼ Credit

If you are a do-it-yourself type and don't want to take donations, you could of course put it on your existing credit card, open a new card, or use credit programs designed just for veterinary care such as CareCredit (*www.carecredit.com*). While you could probably get a better interest rate with a traditional credit card, programs like CareCredit allow an owner to cover expenses with a dedicated line of credit, so payment is simple and focused on veterinary care (once you have the CareCredit you can't go out and shop at the mall as you might with an actual credit card). CareCredit goes directly through your vet. Not all vets offer this program, but in case of emergency, it's worth seeing which ones do.

When It's Not Your Choice

Sometimes you don't get to decide when it's time to say goodbye to your dog. Sometimes they go on their own and alleviate the pain of you making a decision, as happened with one of my absolute favorite girls, Joy, and her beloved Napoleon:

Joy and Nappy

"The last time Nappy slept with me I started to get a sense that he was leaving. He slept in my arms the whole night. I remember the morning of the day that he died, he went in my closet and I said to him, 'If you have to go today, don't stay for me.'"

Joy put his special pillow down in the closet so Nappy had a place to lie down in case he had to go. While Joy desperately wanted to stay home, she had an important meeting to attend; it was literally one of the most important meetings of her career. Knowing she had no choice, she covered little Nappy up with his favorite leopard blanket on his special pillow and walked toward the front door, still unsure of her decision.

Her friend Heather found Nappy "asleep" when she came to let him and his dog-mate Dolly out for their midday romp in the backyard. While Joy misses Nappy greatly, she is so appreciative for the time that they had together. "I still miss him. I miss him every day. I talk about him every day. I will talk about him for the rest of my life. He changed me as a person."

What Happens After?

After your dog has crossed, it is up to you to decide what you want to do with your dog's remains. There are numerous options, and it is best to choose one in advance. Right after it happens, you will be somewhat traumatized and probably unable to make any decisions. Not that your vet is going to do anything shady with your dog, but once you get a little distance on the process, it might be too late to choose your preferred course of action. The options are either cremation or burial.

dealing with the hard stuff

▼ Cremation

Most owners I know have chosen to have their dogs cremated. Your vet will send your dog's remains to a cremation service and call you when you can pick up your dog's ashes. Joy has Nappy's ashes in a beautiful urn on her desk. She sees her Nappy every day, and while she misses him, feels he's always with her.

▼ Burial

You can bring your dog home or to a favorite spot for burial. Just be sure to follow the appropriate city codes in your area. You don't want to have to go through the pain of losing your dog and then get in trouble for how you said goodbye. There are also pet cemeteries as well as some people cemeteries that allow pets to be buried alongside other family members.

What to Do If Your Dog Goes Missing

One of the most unpleasant experiences an owner can face is having her dog go missing. It's an excruciating combination of guilt, panic, and sadness all rolled into one. Here are the best practices for dealing with this trying situation.

Stay Calm

The first thing the owner of a missing dog must do is calm down and stay focused on what you can do, rather than what has happened. While you will of course want to lose it, you must keep it together for your dog's sake. A clear head and your knowledge of your dog's behavior could be essential to finding him.

Make and Post Signs

Signs are an important way to get the word out that your dog is missing. That is how our friend Lucian got his boxer Gumbo back. The more eyes that see your sign the better the chance your dog will come home. But not all signs are created equal. People will be reading these as they drive by, so make yours brief, but specific. If your dog is a Schnauzer, don't just say "LOST." Say "LOST—SCHNAUZER."

Make sure your sign includes the following details:

- A large, clear picture of your dog
- Reward (if you can offer one; see below)
- Breed
- Name (or a nickname he answers to)
- Weight or approximate size
- Gender (if male, whether or not he is altered)
- A description of any distinct markings
- Where the dog was last seen
- A contact number/e-mail address
- The date

Computer-generated signs are preferable to handwritten ones because they are easier to read. Plus, once the sign has been created on a computer you can quickly generate and distribute extra ones.

Once you have created a sign, post it everywhere. For maximum impact, mount your fliers on larger fluorescent poster boards and then post them around the neighborhood. To get the most views, display your signs along busy streets and at high-volume intersections near where your dog got out. Also, once a sign has been created, copy it into an e-mail and ask friends to help spread the word.

Be Available

When a dog is found and she is wearing tags or someone spots a sign and has seen your dog, you must be accessible. Unfortunately, even the most phone obsessed among us can miss a call. To avoid losing a good lead, change your outgoing voicemail: "This is so-and-so and I am temporarily unavailable. If you are calling about my dog, please leave a message here or call me at any time day or night on my cell phone at. . . ."

Reward

Offering a reward, although not absolutely necessary, may encourage more people to keep an eye out for your dog. If you do choose to offer a reward, it's best not to include a specific amount on your flier. This way you can entice people to help your cause, but not advertise that you have X number of dollars lying around. This should help keep some of the crazies away.

Speaking of crazies, while the vast majority of calls that come from lost-dog signs will be from good people wishing to help, it is common for people searching for a lost pet to field a few calls from people with less-than-good intentions. If someone calls saying they have seen your dog and want to meet you in person or they seem overly interested in the reward, be nice, but be suspicious. Ask lots of questions and, if you do choose to meet anyone in person, make sure that you are not alone and meet at a populated place.

Contact Your Local Shelter

A Good Samaritan, not knowing how long a stray has been on the loose, might scoop your dog up and bring it to a shelter within minutes of him getting out. So, be sure to scour your local animal shelters immediately and frequently. While animal-control websites allow you to scan shelters virtually, as do wonderful sites like *www.pets911.com* and *www.petharbor.com*, it's best to visit your local shelters in person. Shelter attendants do their best, but especially in high-volume shelters, they will make mistakes regarding key identifying features such as age, weight, breed, or even gender. This makes online searches for lost pets less effective than visiting the shelter firsthand. Plus, when you go to the shelter, you can both post your sign on the bulletin board and give it to the shelter attendants, kindly asking them to keep an eye out.

Walk the Neighborhood Multiple Times

While dogs can run up to ten miles in a day, many recently escaped dogs will either stay in the area where they feel most comfortable or return to their home turf after a long, sometimes painful journey. Post your fliers around the area in which they were last

DOGMA:

Distance Matters

Check shelters in a sixty-mile radius. Dogs can run five to ten miles in a day and the shelter they end up in may be clear across town.

seen, inform your neighbors, ask your letter carrier, and scour your dog's favorite spots. Does your dog love the park down the street? Does she have a pal in the neighborhood? Are there some particularly stinky garbage dumpsters around the corner? You may get lucky and find your dog lurking about in one of these preferred locales.

The Scene of the Escape

Dogs sometimes attempt to return home on their own, so leave the gate open and don't patch up the hole through which they escaped. Give your dog a pathway back into your yard and some direction on how to get home. Dogs can track scents from blocks away. Leave out some food or something with your smell on it such as a T-shirt or blanket.

The Experts

Expert lost-pet recovery services are cropping up across the country. An owner can hire experts at varying rates to help track

DOGMA:

Lost and Found

Don't hate the dog-catcher. If your dog is lost, try to establish a good rapport with the local animal-control facilities. Animal Control Officers can keep you informed if any dogs matching your pup's description come in.

a dog using techniques ranging from basics, such as posting fliers and keeping track of animals at local shelters, to a more *CSI*-style investigatory approach in which search specialists utilize scent-tracking dogs and even DNA testing to help find your dog. The costs can be high—sometimes thousands of dollars—but these people have extensive experience; plus, the advantage for you is that this is their job and not just a volunteer activity they may have to drop. If you are considering hiring such a service, it's best to do so soon after your dog goes missing. The first twenty-four hours are crucial for these services to track scents and find clues. For more information, go to *www.lostapet.org*.

Avoid Losing Your Dog in the First Place

The best advice I can impart to an owner is to do everything you can to avoid having your dog get out in the first place. Every incident is different, but there are a few universal factors that prevent a dog getting out:

- Neuter your dog
- Check fences for holes
- Limit access to workers and irresponsible friends
- Be realistic about your dog's anxiety level
- Use a no-slip collar or harness when in unfamiliar areas

CANINE CONSIDERATION ❖ ❖ ❖

You are your dog's best protector. Make sure his environment is safe and keep your head when and if he ever gets lost. Your knowledge of your dog's behavior could be the key to finding him and bringing him home.

Unfortunately, even with these preventative techniques in place, dogs still somehow manage to get out. To keep your dog's time away from home as brief as possible, there are specific things you can do.

▼ Pet ID

Having your dog wear an ID tag is an important way to facilitate her quick return. Standard ID tags can be purchased and personalized at the pet store with machines such as Quick Tags or ordered online through websites like *www.pettags.com*. However, a tag is only as good as the information you include. Unfortunately, most tags are limited to a certain number of characters—especially for small dogs' tags—so choose your information wisely. While your dog's name is important, your own name and current contact information are more essential (if you're traveling, be sure you provide a cell number or local contact number).

How far you want to go to enhance your pet's protection is something only you can decide, and with new technology the options are endless. Bella wears a collar embroidered with my last name and contact number in fluorescent letters. Although extremely effective, this is quite low-tech compared to the new tags available, which use GPS technology to track a lost dog just as you track a stolen car.

▼ Microchip Your Dog

Speaking of tracking your dog, remember that microchips are another important tool in reuniting dogs and their owners. Often, the first thing that happens when a dog gets out of his house is his tags or collar falls off. A microchip becomes the only hope an owner has of finding their dog. Dogs can run miles upon miles in a day and owners don't always know which animal-control facilities to check for their dog, but microchips allow a dog to be linked back to his owner no matter how far away he gets.

Microchipping technology is amazing, and it is lifesaving; however, there is a challenge. There are two competitive vendors of microchips—Home Again (*www.homeagain.com*) and Microchip ID Systems (*www.microchipidsystems.com*), but there isn't a scanner that can read both brands of microchips. So, to best protect your dog, contact the shelters in your area to find out which brand of scanners they have.

No matter which service you choose, one thing remains consistent: You must keep the information on that chip up to date. This became clear recently when my dad found a stray dog in the park.

Mars

Mars—we knew his name from the microchip system—a Welsh Springer Spaniel, was running loose in our neighborhood park. He was wearing a collar but no tag. We searched the area but didn't find anyone looking for him or any signs, so I took him to our local after-hours vet hospital to be scanned for a chip. Indeed, he was chipped, but his microchip information gave his contact as one of three options: a disconnected number, the exchange of a large cancer hospital fifty miles away, and a voicemail with no name. Between the various numbers, I must have left about twenty messages, but it was getting late and we were getting nowhere. I left Mars at the vet and went home to get some sleep. The next morning the owners called my dad, overjoyed that we had found their—get this—prizewinning dog! Mars's pedigree was a million miles long, and his owners had been up all night searching for him. They had been visiting their mother's house in our area, and Mars slipped out when a gardener left the gate open. The couple had placed signs (which we missed) around the neighborhood, but because they hadn't remembered that Mars was chipped, they didn't think to check their work telephone numbers, which were the ones listed through the chip system. Thankfully, Mars made it home safe and sound, and he now wears a collar embroidered with his owner's cell phone number in bold lettering.

▼ License Your Dog—Make It Official

Many jurisdictions require you to license your dog. Although getting licensed may seem like a hassle, the license tag on your dog's collar tells anyone who sees your dog that she belongs to someone. Dog licenses usually feature a distinct number, so if your dog is found your information is on file and you can be located.

eleven

final thoughts

Now, if I was reading this book and came to the end, I know I'd be a bit overwhelmed. And the last thing I ever want to do with this book is overwhelm anyone. I want all owners and owners-to-be out there to raise wonderful dogs and not drive themselves crazy in the process. That said, I know there is a lot to think about and keep track of. So, here is a quick cheat sheet of some extremely important points in a format that even an addled owner like myself can appreciate.

Do:

- **Keep your dog up to date on vaccines.** This keeps him healthy and you able to board him for that last-minute rendezvous.

- **Spay or neuter your dog.** This keeps her healthy, pet over-population down, and you from being an owner of multiple puppies.

- **Crate train your dog.** It's the basis of being a good dog owner.

- **Feed your dog high-quality dog food.** This keeps your dog's coat soft, his shedding down, and your vet bills lower.

- **Take your dog everywhere (if she enjoys it).** Celebrate spending your free time with her.

- **Choose the right dog for your lifestyle.** You want to enjoy being an owner, not a slave to the wrong kind of dog.

- **Consider rescue.** Rescue dogs are deeply appreciative of you, and many come potty trained!

- **Make sure your dog has access to clean water.** Dogs, like people, need water to thrive.

- **Start off on the right foot.** Get a trainer the first weekend you get a dog.

- **Treat your vet office staff like gold.** You'll come to need them one day.

- **Check references for vets, kennels, and dog walkers.** These people are caring for your pooch. Take the time to check them out.

- **Give your dog interactive treats such as Kongs or Marrow Bones.** It keeps them busy and away from your shoes.

Don't:

- **Be careless with a retractable leash.** They are a privilege, not a right. Some dogs need more control than a retractable leash provides and all dogs need to be better controlled on busy streets.
- **Walk your dog off-leash.** Ever seen a dead dog on a leash? Harsh, but true. Even the best-behaved dogs are dogs and might chase a squirrel, cat, or another dog right into traffic.
- **Overreact to situations.** Your dog will follow your lead.
- **Buy a dog from a pet store, classified ad, or an online facility that you haven't personally inspected.** Many of these dogs come from puppy mills where they are kept under deplorable circumstances.
- **Be a mindless dog owner.** Not everyone loves dogs, and it's your responsibility to watch your dog's behavior.
- **Choose a dog based on looks alone.** You might end up with a bad match.
- **Pay too much for pet supplies like beds, crates, and leashes.** Search the Internet for deals.
- **Leave a dog in the car for extended periods of time, or at all if the temperature exceeds 70°F.** Thousands of dogs die each year from heat exhaustion after being left in hot cars.
- **Assume all dogs are as well behaved or friendly as yours.** Ask if a dog is friendly, and keep a healthy distance until you get a good feeling from the owner.
- **Ignore your instincts regarding your dog's health, a vet, a kennel, or a dog walker.** If something is off, it's your responsibility to do a little investigating.

final thoughts

Make your dog codependent. You may have to travel or have your dog sleep in a crate when you travel. Don't end up with a dog that melts down unless you're holding him every second.

Finally, the most important *don't* of all:

Don't ever let the perfect be the enemy of the good.

You're not going to do everything perfectly perfect every time. You will most likely, at one point or another, think that you are a crappy owner. You won't always make it home every three hours on the dot to let your puppy out to pee. You will probably forget one month to put flea and tick goo on your dog. You definitely will go overboard buying stuff for your dog that you totally don't need. And you absolutely will ignore or forget a lot of what is in this book. That's all pretty much okay—within reason, of course.

It comes down to this. Unless you really are a crappy dog owner—which I'm sure you won't be—you're going to have to learn how to take a big step back and say, "I did my best, and that's all I can do." And here's the best part: In your dog's eyes—no matter what you forgot, what you did wrong, or who dumped you—you're perfect!

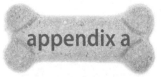

resources

Researching a Breed and Making a Mutt Map

The American Kennel Club (*www.akc.org*)

Australian Shepherd Club of America *(www.asca.org)*

Dog Breed Info Center (*www.dogbreedinfo.com/search.htm*)

Dog Breed Selection Quiz (*http://animal.discovery.com
/breedselector/dogselectorindex.do*)

Dogster (*www.dogster.com*)

Elite Pets Internet Club (*http://zooclub.biz/dog_breeds*)

The Papillon Club of American (*www.Papillonclub.org*)

The Partnership for Animal Welfare, Pet Bull Corner
(*www.paw-rescue.org/petbulls.html*)

Finding a Dog

Adopt a Pet.com (*www.adoptapet.com*)

Beauty & Beast Kennels (*www.beautynbeast.net*)

Dogster (*www.dogster.com*)

The Humane Society of America (*www.hsus.org*)

Petfinder (*www.petfinder.com*)

Pet Harbor (*www.petharbor.com*)

Senior Dog Project (*www.srdogs.com*)

Stop Puppy Mills: The Humane Society of the United States
(*www.stoppuppymills.org*)

Training

Pet Place.com (*www.petplace.com/dogs/crate-training -problems/page1.aspx*)

Tamar Geller (*www.tamargeller.com*)

Training as a Team L.A. (*www.trainingasateamla.com*)

Health Care

American Academy of Veterinary Acupuncture (*www.aava.org*)

American Holistic Veterinary Medical Association (*www.ahvma.org*)

American Veterinary Medical Association (*www.avma.org*)

BarfWorld (*www.barfworld.com*)

The Dog Food Project (*www.dogfoodproject.com*)

HealthyPetNet (*www.healthypetsonline.com*)

International Veterinary Acupuncture Society (*www.ivas.org*)

North Shore Animal League (*www.spayusa.org*)

Petcare Insurance (*http://petcareinsurance.com/us /dog-insurance-gold.asp*)

Pet Education.com (*www.peteducation.com*)

Veterinary Oral Health Council (*www.vohc.org*)

Dog Care Products

FURminator De-shedding Products (*www.furminator.com*)

The Orvis Company (*www.orvis.com*)

Pet Street Mall (*www.petstreetmall.com*)

Traveling Tips

American Airlines, "Traveling with Pets" (*www.aa.com /content/travelInformation/specialAssistance /travelingWithPets.jhtml*)

Border Collie Rescue (*www.bcrescue.org/flying.html*)

DogFriendly.com (*www.dogfriendly.com*)

Kimpton Hotels (*www.kimptonhotels.com*)

Pacific Pet Transport (*www.pacpet.com*)

Pet Flight (*www.petflight.com*)

Pet Travel.com (*www.pettravel.com*)

Sherpa (*www.sherpapet.com*)

Transportation Security Administration (*www.tsa.gov
/travelers/airtravel/assistant/editorial_1036.shtm*)

Financing Care

Angels 4 Animals (*www.angels4animals.org*)

Best Friends Animal Society (*www.bestfriends.org*)

CareCredit (*www.carecredit.com*)

Cavy Care Inc. Guinea Pig Shelter and Sanctuary
(*www.cavycareinc.org/help_w_vet_bills.htm*)

Petcare Insurance (*http://petcareinsurance.com/us
/dog-insurance-gold.asp*)

The Pet Fund (*www.thepetfund.com*)

Finding Lost Dogs

HomeAgain (*www.homeagain.com*)

Microchip ID Systems (*www.microchipidsystems.com*)

Missing Pet Partnership: Search and Rescue for Lost Pets
(*www.lostapet.org*)

Pets 911 (*www.pets911.com*)

Pet Tags.com (*www.pettags.com*)

Grief Counseling and Support

Pet Loss Grief Support Website (*www.petloss.com*)

Pet Loss Support Hotline Center for Companion Animal
Health (*www.vetmed.ucdavis.edu/petloss/index.htm*)

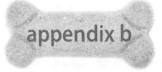

AKC breed chart

THE SPORTING GROUP

Breed	Max Height	Max Weight	Reality Check
American Water Spaniel	18 inches	45 pounds	Can develop chewing and digging habits
Brittany	20 inches	40 pounds	Will become nervous and hyperactive if not given lots of exercise
Chesapeake Bay Retriever	26 inches	80 pounds	Sheds a lot; never lets a puddle go to waste
Clumber Spaniel	19 inches	85 pounds	Can develop joint problems
Cocker Spaniel	15 inches	30 pounds	Needs gentle care; should not sleep outside
Curly-Coated Retriever	27 inches	40 pounds	Can be a bit stubborn
English Cocker Spaniel	16 inches	30 pounds	Has a tendency to bark if not properly trained
English Setter	26 inches	70 pounds	
English Springer Spaniel	20 inches	50 pounds	Needs exercise or will become overweight
Field Spaniel	19 inches	55 pounds	Needs extra care on ears and coat
Flat-Coated Retriever	25 inches	70 pounds	Very energetic and strong, needs lots of exercise

THE SPORTING GROUP (*continued*)

Breed	Max Height	Max Weight	Reality Check
German Shorthaired Pointer	23 inches	70 pounds	Needs to be outside a lot to be truly happy
German Wirehaired Pointer	26 inches	80 pounds	Will demand long walks
Golden Retriever	24 inches	75 pounds	Needs lots of exercise
Gordon Setter	27 inches	80 pounds	Big, hairy dog—needs lots of brushing
Irish Setter	27 inches	75 pounds	Needs extra grooming, exercise, and training
Irish Water Spaniel	24 inches	65 pounds	Can be very hyper
Labrador Retriever	25 inches	80 pounds	Possibly the most hyper puppies in the universe; adults usually settle down
Pointer	28 inches	75 pounds	Needs and loves the active life
Spinone Italiano	28 inches	85 pounds	Too laid back for active sorts, needs too much exercise for others
Sussex Spaniel	15 inches	45 pounds	Needs a fair amount of grooming and exercise
Vizsla	24 inches	60 pounds	Requires gentle handling
Weimaraner	27 inches	85 pounds	Will try to become the alpha member of the household
Welsh Springer Spaniel	20 inches	50 pounds	Craves lots of attention
Wirehaired Pointing Griffon	24 inches	70 pounds	Needs lots of grooming

THE HOUND GROUP

Breed	Max Height	Max Weight	Reality Check
Afghan Hound	27 inches	60 pounds	Requires extensive grooming; can be destructive if too bored
Basenji	17 inches	25 pounds	Requires lots of patience when training
Basset Hound	14 inches	55 pounds	When these usually laidback dogs catch a scent, just try and stop them from following it
Beagle	15 inches	30 pounds	Very spunky, very curious, and likes to bark
Black and Tan Coonhound	27 inches	100 pounds	Tends to run off "on the hunt" if loose
Bloodhound	27 inches	110 pounds	Can be shy
Borzoi	28 inches	105 pounds	Needs lots of exercise; sheds a lot
Dachshund (Standard)	18 inches	20 pounds	Prone to spinal damage from jumping and falling
Foxhound, American	25 inches	70 pounds	Needs lots of exercise
Foxhound, English	24 inches	65 pounds	Happiest in rural areas
Greyhound	30 inches	70 pounds	Will chew on things if not extensively exercised; somewhat fragile
Harrier	21 inches	55 pounds	Doesn't like to be alone
Ibizan Hound	28 inches	55 pounds	Can jump over most short fences
Irish Wolfhound	34 inches	135 pounds	As fast as he is big, needs space and attention
Norwegian Elkhound	21 inches	60 pounds	Needs lots of grooming and weekly baths

AKC breed chart

THE HOUND GROUP (*continued*)

Breed	Max Height	Max Weight	Reality Check
Otterhound	27 inches	120 pounds	Likes to howl
Petit Basset Griffon Vendéen	15 inches	35 pounds	Can be noisy
Pharaoh Hound	25 inches	60 pounds	Often wary of strange children
Rhodesian Ridgeback	27 inches	85 pounds	Requires extra training
Saluki	28 inches	65 pounds	Prone to some health problems
Scottish Deerhound	33 inches	120 pounds	A big dog that fares best living indoors
Whippet	22 inches	28 pounds	Can be shy

THE WORKING GROUP

Breed	Max Height	Max Weight	Reality Check
Akita	28 inches	105 pounds	Lots of shedding; can be aggressive; a fenced yard is highly recommended
Alaskan Malamute	25 inches	75 pounds	Very strong and energetic
Anatolian Shepherd	32 inches	140 pounds	Wary around strange people and dogs, but very gentle in general
Bernese Mountain Dog	28 inches	90 pounds	Needs lots of brushing and exercise
Boxer	25 inches	80 pounds	Adventurous, likes to get loose and run around
Bull Mastiff	27 inches	130 pounds	A very large and powerful dog that needs a firm master

Breed	Max Height	Max Weight	Reality Check
Doberman Pinscher	28 inches	85 pounds	Although easy to train, if not trained properly, the results can be disastrous
Giant Schnauzer	28 inches	85 pounds	Requires frequent professional grooming
Great Dane	32+ inches	120 pounds	Needs lots of attention, very big and strong
Great Pyrenees	32 inches	130 pounds	Requires extensive socializing (otherwise can be overly protective)
Greater Swiss Mountain Dog	29 inches	135 pounds	Has a history of joint and blood disorders
Komondor	28 inches	105 pounds	Independent minded; requires diligent and extensive grooming
Kuvasz	30 inches	115 pounds	Sheds a lot; needs lots of exercise
Mastiff	34 inches	220 pounds	Huge! Although very gentle, can be dangerous in rough play
Newfoundland	30 inches	150 pounds	Needs to be outdoors, loves water
Portuguese Water Dog	23 inches	60 pounds	Will demand attention
Rottweiler	27 inches	110 pounds	Can be dangerous without proper training
Saint Bernard	28 inches	135 pounds	Although gentle, its sheer size can make it a danger to small children
Samoyed	24 inches	65 pounds	Needs lots of grooming

THE WORKING GROUP (*continued*)

Breed	Max Height	Max Weight	Reality Check
Siberian Husky	24 inches	65 pounds	Sheds constantly; loves and needs to run
Standard Schnauzer	20 inches	50 pounds	Very energetic; can jump high fences

THE TERRIER GROUP

Breed	Max Height	Max Weight	Reality Check
Airedale Terrier	23 inches	45 pounds	Requires frequent, often difficult, grooming
American Staffordshire Terrier	19 inches	50 pounds	Originally bred as a fighting dog; requires extensive socializing
Australian Terrier	11 inches	15 pounds	Can be aggressive or shy toward strangers
Bedlington Terrier	17 inches	23 pounds	Needs daily grooming
Border Terrier	15 inches	16 pounds	Needs more than average grooming; can be assertive
Bull Terrier	16 inches	40 pounds	Needs lots of companionship
Cairn Terrier	10 inches	15 pounds	Needs a firm, strong master
Dandie Dinmont Terrier	11 inches	24 pounds	Very independent minded
Fox Terrier (Smooth)	16 inches	19 pounds	Sheds more than average; can be hyperactive
Fox Terrier (Wirehaired)	16 inches	20 pounds	Very energetic and sometimes mischievous
Irish Terrier	18 inches	30 pounds	Has a tendency to run into things possibly causing injury or damage

Breed	Max Height	Max Weight	Reality Check
Jack Russell Terrier	14 inches	17 pounds	Known to dominate households
Kerry Blue Terrier	20 inches	40 pounds	Needs a hair trimming every couple of months
Lakeland Terrier	15 inches	18 pounds	
Manchester Terrier (Standard)	Varies	7–22 pounds	Can be noisy
Miniature Bull Terrier	14 inches	20 pounds	Mischievous
Miniature Schnauzer	14 inches	15 pounds	Needs lots of grooming
Norfolk Terrier	10 inches	12 pounds	Doesn't do well alone
Norwich Terrier	10 inches	12 pounds	Perhaps too brave for its own good sometimes
Scottish Terrier	10 inches	22 pounds	Often bad tempered
Sealyham Terrier	11 inches	25 pounds	Independent nature
Skye Terrier	10 inches	25 pounds	Can sometimes be aloof
Soft Coated Wheaten Terrier	19 inches	40 pounds	Acts like a puppy for its entire life
Staffordshire Bull Terrier	16 inches	38 pounds	Needs lots of exercise to stay in shape
Welsh Terrier	16 inches	23 pounds	Requires a fair amount of grooming and baths
West Highland White Terrier	12 inches	22 pounds	Can be dominating

THE NON-SPORTING GROUP

Breed	Max Height	Max Weight	Reality Check
American Eskimo Dog	19 inches	35 pounds	Requires regular, often difficult brushing
Bichon Frisé	12 inches	14 pounds	Requires frequent grooming

THE NON-SPORTING GROUP (*continued*)

Breed	Max Height	Max Weight	Reality Check
Boston Terrier	12 inches	25 pounds	Must be kept indoors; sensitive to extreme temperatures
Bulldog	16 inches	50 pounds	Will need daily face-wrinkle cleanings
Chinese Shar-Pei	20 inches	60 pounds	Often does not get along with other animals
Chow Chow	20 inches	70 pounds	Needs more than average amount of grooming
Dalmatian	23 inches	70 pounds	Very strong and active; needs a fenced yard
Finnish Spitz	20 inches	35 pounds	Can be noisy
French Bulldog	12 inches	28 pounds	Expensive to buy and own
Keeshond	18 inches	65 pounds	Lots of fur, which won't all stay on the dog
Lhasa Apso	11 inches	16 pounds	Likes to bark at the slightest suspicious sound
Löwchen	14 inches	18 pounds	Requires lots of grooming
Poodle (Standard)	15 inches	65 pounds	Very active
Schipperke	13 inches	16 pounds	Although very fluffy, their coats are not very soft
Shiba Inu	17 inches	25 pounds	Can be a bit nervous
Tibetan Spaniel	10 inches	15 pounds	Shouldn't be left alone for any considerable period
Tibetan Terrier	16 inches	30 pounds	Requires frequent grooming; can be shy

THE HERDING GROUP

Breed	Max Height	Max Weight	Reality Check
Australian Cattle Dog	20 inches	50 pounds	Absolutely tireless
Australian Shepherd	23 inches	60 pounds	Needs lots of brushing; prone to hip dysplasia
Bearded Collie	22 inches	60 pounds	Needs lots of exercise and preferably room to run
Belgian Malinois	26 inches	80 pounds	Somewhat sensitive, high strung, and prone to separation anxiety
Belgian Sheepdog	26 inches	75 pounds	Needs lots of space and exercise; needs more than average grooming
Belgian Tervuren	17 inches	23 pounds	Requires daily, albeit quick, grooming
Border Collie	22 inches	55 pounds	Fast, playful, and will never be too tired
Bouvier des Flandres	28 inches	120 pounds	A big dog that sheds a lot
Briard	27 inches	120 pounds	Will try (and usually succeed) to herd you and your children
Canaan Dog	24 inches	55 pounds	Independent minded
Collie	26 inches	75 pounds	Requires more than average grooming
German Shepherd Dog	26 inches	85 pounds	Very big and very active
Old English Sheepdog	25 inches	70 pounds	Sheds a lot
Puli	17 inches	35 pounds	Difficult and time consuming to bathe
Shetland Sheepdog	16 inches	27 pounds	Barks more than average
Welsh Corgi, Cardigan	12 inches	38 pounds	Sheds more than average
Welsh Corgi, Pembroke	12 inches	30 pounds	Sheds a lot; needs extra brushing

AKC breed chart

THE COMPLETE AKC TOY GROUP

Breed	Max Height	Max Weight	Reality Check
Affenpinscher	11 inches	9 pounds	Will not be ignored
Brussels Griffon	10 inches	12 pounds	Will demand lots of attention
Cavalier King Charles Spaniel	13 inches	18 pounds	Difficult to find (rare)
Chihuahua	5 inches	6 pounds	Too fragile for outdoor living
Chinese Crested	13 inches	12 pounds	Hairless—needs lotion in dry weather, or for the sun
English Toy Spaniel	10 inches	14 pounds	Requires more than average brushing
Havanese	11 inches	13 pounds	Sometimes overly friendly
Italian Greyhound	15 inches	13 pounds	Sensitive to the cold
Japanese Chin	11 inches	7 pounds	Sensitive and sometimes finicky
Maltese	10 inches	7 pounds	Requires daily brushing
Manchester Terrier (Toy)	12 inches	12 pounds	Barks more than average
Miniature Pinscher	12 inches	12 pounds	Barks a lot
Papillon	11 inches	10 pounds	Prone to eye problems
Pekingese	9 inches	14 pounds	Stubborn
Pomeranian	11 inches	7 pounds	Can be demanding and somewhat hyper
Poodle (Toy)	10 inches	15 pounds	Can be hyper
Pug	11 inches	18 pounds	Craves lots of attention
Shih Tzu	10 inches	16 pounds	Requires extensive daily grooming
Silky Terrier	10 inches	11 pounds	Needs a brief daily brushing; somewhat fragile
Yorkshire Terrier	7 inches	7 pounds	Fragile

THE MISCELLANEOUS CLASS

Breed	Max Height	Max Weight	Reality Check
German Pinscher	20 inches	35 pounds	Not recommended for homes with children
Plott Hound	25 inches	60 pounds	Has a very loud bark
Polish Lowland Sheepdog	20 inches	80 pounds	Needs firm training
Toy Fox Terrier	11 inches	7 pounds	Very energetic

about the author

Betsy Rosenfeld is the go-to girl in Los Angeles when it comes to all things dog. She has dedicated her life to rescuing dogs, working with both local L.A.-based rescues as well as international animal aid organizations. She is a regional council member of IFAW (The International Fund for Animal Welfare), and she helped raise critical funds for the group's post–Hurricane Katrina rescue efforts.

Betsy is also an accomplished writer-producer. Her work ranges from producing the acclaimed Sundance feature *Grand Theft Parsons* starring Johnny Knoxville and Christina Applegate to her latest project, Video Voter—a new media nonpartisan initiative to educate voters with short videos (*www.videovoter.org*). The *Wall Street Journal* recently profiled Rosenfeld as an expert for her work on Video Voter, for which she has written an acclaimed, in-depth guidebook titled *Video Voter: Producing Election Coverage for Your Community*.

Rosenfeld has now combined her skills and her passion for working with dogs to launch *www.LOVETHYDOG.com*, a vibrant website offering dog lovers information on how to care for their precious pooches. Betsy lives in Beverly Hills with her favorite dog, Bella, whom she found running in traffic.

index